Business School

Management, Inquiry and Action

Caroline Ramsey

This publication forms part of the Open University module B204 *Making it happen! Leadership, influence and change*. Details of this and other Open University modules can be obtained from the Student Registration and Enquiry Service, The Open University, PO Box 197, Milton Keynes MK7 6BJ, United Kingdom (tel. +44 (0)845 300 60 90; email general-enquiries@open.ac.uk).

Alternatively, you may visit the Open University website at www.open.ac.uk where you can learn more about the wide range of modules and packs offered at all levels by The Open University.

To purchase a selection of Open University materials visit www.ouw.co.uk, or contact Open University Worldwide, Walton Hall, Milton Keynes MK7 6AA, United Kingdom for a catalogue (tel. +44 (0)1908 858785; fax +44 (0)1908 858779; email ouw-customer-services@open.ac.uk).

The Open University, Walton Hall, Milton Keynes MK7 6AA

First published 2013. Adapted from *Introducing Reflective Learning* (2008) ISBN 978 1 8487 3395 4 and *Developing Productive Inquiry* (2008) ISBN 978 1 8487 3450 0

Edited and designed by The Open University.

Typeset by The Open University.

Printed in the United Kingdom by Charlesworth Press, Wakefield.

ISBN 978 1 7800 7437 5

1.1

Management, Inquiry and Action

Caroline Ramsey

Contents

Preface

Preface

At the heart of management learning lies inquiry: the asking of questions. These questions can be straightforward, 'Have sales increased this month?' or they can be complicated with answers that will always be ambivalent, for example, 'How can I get a team of very different people to work together?' The latter question is likely to need a slightly different answer on most days! Because so many of the questions a manager has to answer are complex, with answers that are frequently equivocal, time and thought will need to be given to interpreting the answers that we work with. This time and thought is called reflection.

Reflection in its many guises

It is commonly said that the study of management is a reflective practice. If you are studying management and business in some formal programme then it is likely that you will be encouraged on several occasions to engage in reflective learning, but what does this mean? Well, the problem in defining reflective learning is that reflection can refer to several activities that are closely related but not exactly the same thing and nothing is more confusing in life than when somebody nearly means the same as you but not quite the same!

Here are three possible understandings of the activity of reflection:

1   Reflection can be the process by which you use your experience to help you understand and apply academic ideas, such as theories, frameworks or models. It often helps in understanding a new idea if you can relate it to an experience and see how that idea would help you in similar situations.

2   Reflection can also be a process by which you learn from experience in a more personal way. So, for example, as you reflect on an event you might be able to see how your values shaped your actions and, perhaps, consider if your values might need updating or if you need to be more open with colleagues about what matters to you.

3   Finally, reflection can be the process by which you pause and think about what you should do next. It will involve you thinking about

what is going on, what needs your action, where can you act on your own and where you need support from others.

In this book we will consider understandings 2 and 3 from the list above, but we will focus predominantly on the third understanding of reflection. The goal of this book will be to consider the question 'What should I do next?'

Productive inquiry?

A key feature of this book is that inquiry is a crucial practice for a manager. Linked to that, is a belief that inquiry is not merely a case of asking questions about the world, but is also a process by which we can explore what sort of a world, or organisation, we can make. Inquiry is not just about discovery it is also generative. It generates possible actions, likely relations and potential reaction. Inquiry is to a manager what hammering is to a carpenter or taking a temperature is to a doctor: a crucial practice that is a central part of doing the job well.

And what role does inquiry play for a manager? It provides the substance upon which a manager can reflect; without a serious practice of inquiry reflection can become little more than anecdote, assumption or prejudice. It is inquiry that enables a manager to challenge their own, or their colleagues' taken for granted blinkers. It is inquiry that brings a manager hard up against the tricky problems that she or he must handle. It is a practice of inquiry that can keep a manager alert to situations that need innovation, change or development. This book is a part of a module on leadership and change management. Do you want to lead? Do you want to initiate changes that will benefit yourself and your organisation? If so, you can kiss goodbye to any hopes of sustainable success without an ongoing practice of inquiry.

The book structure

So in Part 1 of this book we look at three models of reflection. Perhaps the best known model that we look at is David Kolb's (1984) model of learning from experience, although we will use his model in a slightly different manner to how he originally intended. His original goal was to design a way for including experience in formal courses of academic learning. We will be using his model to help us think about how we go about working and managing with our organisations and also how we might act in particular situations.

Then, in Part 2, we look closely at how we can gather the material, or evidence, upon which we will base our reflections and actions. We will work through how to design and carry out a high quality inquiry and how to interpret and understand the data that we gather.

Inquiry and action

One final, short comment to make about inquiry; it is not just about gathering information before we act. We are not going to learn how to be academic researchers, nor will we want to engage in analysis paralysis. There are occasions when managers need to conduct their inquiry *after* taking action, asking 'Did it work?' Often taking action is the only way of finding the information that we need.

So, this book isn't a sort of academic hoop that you need to jump through. Inquiry and the skills you need to conduct good inquiry will be a crucial building block to any managerial career.

I do hope that you enjoy reading, learning and trying out the ideas.

Caroline Ramsey

Part 1: 1 What is 'reflective learning'?

I was talking to a friend recently and he asked me what I was planning to do over the weekend. 'Oh,' I said, 'I've got to write about reflective learning.' Richard gave me a quizzical look and asked me what that was. I wonder if, when you picked up this book, you asked the same question. For some people, the idea of reflecting upon what you have done and thinking about how you could do better next time will seem a natural activity. And yet there is more to reflective learning than that, so it is important to spend a short time at the start of this book thinking about what a regular, thoughtful practice of reflecting on how we do our jobs, live in a family or relate with others might include. To start this process, have a look now at Activity 1.1.

Activity 1.1

5 minutes

Can you think of an occasion that had a major effect on you? Pause for a moment or two and then write down what happened and how you feel you changed as a result.

Comment

Did you find that easy or difficult to do? I remembered an incident about a year ago. I had always enjoyed teaching undergraduate management classes but a project had taken me away for a couple of years to work with managers in a major engineering company. So, last September, I found myself back in a classroom again, teaching management theory to young undergraduates who did not have any work experience. This time I found it very difficult to work just with book theory; I wanted to work with managers who had particular issues that they had to deal with and use my knowledge of management theory to help them. You see, I had changed over the two years, and what once was interesting and enjoyable had palled. I also realised that I was more and more interested in research and reflective learning. It was time to change jobs.

One strange thing about that experience was that I didn't realise what was happening at the time. It took a few weeks for me to notice something was different and then I stopped and thought about it for a few minutes, trying to work out what was going on.

At its very simplest, reflective learning is a deliberate process of undertaking what we will call *cycles of inquiry.* The term 'cycle' is used to capture the way a reflective learner moves between action and reflection. As you can see from the diagram below, there is a sense in which taking action will result in our doing things differently and we can then reflect on what happened next. The reflection should lead to action and so we 'cycle' between action and reflection.

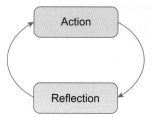

Figure 1.1 The action–reflection cycle

A key word here is 'deliberate'. I'm sure that at some time or other we have thought about what we have just done and wondered how else we could have acted. It is a somewhat different process, however, to set about improving our work or life performance on purpose by actively considering how we should act, then designing and carrying out a new action before stepping back to consider if the new action has made a difference. This, then, is when everyday reflection becomes a serious practice of learning. This is when we can change the way we live and work.

Tom's story

I guess that I'm not very different to any stepdad. I just struggled getting along with my wife's eight-year-old daughter. It didn't matter what I tried, I was always compared unfavourably with her dad and very clearly given the message that I wasn't her 'real' dad. This was especially the case whenever I tried to bring some discipline into our lives. I thought long and hard about how I could improve the situation, how I could show Amy that I was on her side – that I wanted us to create our own relationship not a replacement 'dad' relationship.

I knew that Amy was very keen on nature and so one weekend I suggested that we went to the local nature reserve. Slightly reluctantly, Amy agreed. I did a whole load of searching on the web to find out about the place before we went. The day wasn't a complete disaster – we had some good times but I guess that Amy could see right through me. Nature really isn't my thing; I'm an engineer.

I thought about it a bit more. Somehow, it seemed to me, I had to find a way of creating a relationship that didn't imitate what Amy thought of as her relationship with her dad. I wasn't sure what to do but I decided to look out for opportunities. Actually, I didn't have to wait long. A week or so later, Amy and I were watching a news programme about global warming and energy use. In particular, it mentioned that fitting valves onto individual radiators could save a large amount of energy. Amy was pretty keen on this; apparently her class had discussed it in a recent science lesson. So, I asked her what she knew about it and whether it was something we could do at home. She disappeared upstairs to her room and brought down her school notes. We talked about it for a while and I asked if she would help me sort out our central heating. The next weekend we set off together to the DIY shop, Amy giving me some 'advice' as to what to buy and acting as my plumber's mate, with me using my plumbing skills to change all the radiators.

Was this a breakthrough for Amy and me? I don't know, but it was a good day, when we enjoyed being with each other and doing something together.

Activity 1.2

10 minutes

Tom's is such an ordinary story; I suspect that many of us have been in similar situations. I wonder, however, how many of us would have thought that we were doing some learning then – we tend to pass through such tricky times and put it down to experience. Well, this type of experience can be a source of learning.

1   I mentioned above about going through cycles of inquiry, where action is followed by reflection. Can you see in Tom's story two cycles of inquiry? Note down Tom's two actions and two reflections.

2   Now, think back to a time when you have done something similar either at work or at home.

3   Finally, think of some current situation where some deliberate reflective work might be helpful.

Comment

Tom's first cycle of inquiry was when he considered how to do something with Amy that she would enjoy. The action was to take her to a nature reserve. This outing led to further reflection as Tom realised that this action had not created the hoped-for improvement in relations. The outcome of this reflection was the aim of finding some shared activity that wouldn't mean that Amy compared him unfavourably with her father. The action from this reflection was not so obvious: Tom chose to look out for opportunities to do something new, something that would work for them.

It is worth making a couple of points here which I will return to later on. First, notice Tom's aim to look out for new opportunities. An important part of reflective learning is a growing awareness of what is going on around you. Second, notice how Tom had to wait for an opportunity. We don't control everything and so, as you will see in the section called 'Including others in our reflection', we have to learn how to be aware of the impact of others on our actions.

Creating new actions through thinking reflectively

If one important aspect of reflective learning is that it is deliberate, then a second, and related, aspect is that it is focused on the future. It's all very well looking back on an event and wishing that we had acted differently or saying, 'If that happened again, I'd act differently.' We all know that things never happen the same way twice! So, for learning to happen, you need to use your thinking to affect future actions. The three points you need to consider are:

- generating and evaluating new ideas
- reflecting upon events and situations
- reflecting upon relations.

Generating and evaluating new ideas

This is an important point. Too often managers in organisations, when faced with difficult problems, resort to 'just trying harder'. A crucial part of learning is doing things differently and being able to evaluate the success of these new practices. This point takes us back to my earlier comment about reflective learning being a deliberate practice, with a conscious decision about testing our learning through cycles of inquiry. So, how can you generate new ideas? How can you handle those ideas in order to use them for your learning? One source of new ideas is reading books or thoughtful articles. Not everyone finds reading, especially academic books, easy. I suspect that is because, especially when it has involved reading for learning, we have tended to try and memorise what we read. That makes reading a really hard graft. However, when you read with your eye on how you do your job, then you are not looking to understand every detail; you are looking out for what strikes you, what moves you or what intrigues you. You are looking for possibilities, for ideas that might just work in your life.

Activity 1.3

15 minutes, with a few days to put the idea into practice

1   Go back over the first few pages of this book and see if you can find one suggestion that might offer you a way of doing things differently at work. Make a note of it here.

2   Now think of when you could make this change and how you would know if it had been helpful or not.

Comment

Well done – you have successfully set up your first cycle of inquiry!

There are other ways of getting ideas – from television programmes, conversations or even just going out for a walk. Sometimes we have to avoid being efficient in order to learn! We all need space to think and wonder and that sort of space is often in very short supply, so you will have to make it for yourself.

Reflecting upon events and situations

I'll be dealing with this topic in much greater depth in the next few chapters of this book. It is important to mention here that time is a major issue in reflective learning. We need to make time to consider what has happened and what we can learn from it to shape our own future actions.

Reflecting upon relations

Sometimes we tend to consider only our own actions and think about what difference they might make. However, I would suggest that even when we are trying to do something on our own, the actions of others will limit or help what we are trying to do. Relations, therefore, are crucially important and paying attention to how they develop is a vital reflective skill. I will return to this in more detail later.

What do we reflect on?

So what will be the object of our reflection? How can we put frames around parts of our lives so that we can consider them more carefully?

Frames

You will see this term quite frequently throughout this book. 'Framing' is the act of putting boundaries around events or thoughts to give them a clear focus. For example, you might watch a tennis match and frame it in different ways: you might focus on how to play a backhand shot, or on how to play at the net, or on how to be an umpire. Depending on how you frame the match, you will see very different things.

Framing can be very important to how we learn reflectively as it will determine what we can learn and what events we are likely to notice.

For our purposes, I will suggest three possibilities:

- critical incidents
- a period of time
- an ongoing issue as a focus of inquiry.

Critical incidents

These are situations or events that are, in some way, memorable and significant to us. In particular, look out for incidents where your assumptions about people or the world are challenged or where your current way of working appears to be less than effective. Pay attention to any feelings that something is not quite right, but don't just look for problems: notice the occasions when you catch yourself saying 'if only…' or the times when you feel that if you could do 'that' then you could also do something else. Whatever the prompt, you need to sensitise yourself to the feeling or thought that an event or situation is worth considering at greater length.

Sensitise: this is a process of being more aware of what's going on around us or being sensitive to the possible importance of those events.

Activity 1.4

8 minutes

Jot down some possible 'critical incidents' from your home or working life over the last month.

Comment

Use the information above to help remind you what would indicate a critical incident. Think especially of those times when you thought 'if only…' or where you thought that you could do better next time.

Critical incidents are probably the most common form of reflective learning and you will notice that at least two of the reflective frameworks I introduce later will use critical incidents. The benefit is that critical incidents can provide a clear time boundary around events and a clear focus on a topic of learning. This, however, can also be its weakness as sometimes those boundaries become blinkers.

A period of time

Many people keep a journal of some sort and so reflect back upon how the day or week has gone. Doing this sort of regular reflection can often help us note and give time to consider critical incidents that happen during the day. For me, I find that keeping a journal helps me notice themes and issues that are important to me but which are like undercurrents that I don't notice until I read back on a few days' journal entries and see them coming up. In this way, I can counter the problem of blinkers that I noted in the Comment to Activity 1.4.

Activity 1.5

5 minutes

Do you have any experiences of keeping a journal or diary? When have you used them and how useful have they been?

Comment

So, are your experiences of keeping a journal positive? I must admit that I sometimes find them difficult to maintain but I'm always aware of the benefits when I do keep a journal. That's especially the case when I keep a journal to track my inquiry into a particular topic focus. We will look at this form of reflective thinking next.

An ongoing issue as a focus of inquiry

Here the focus of your reflection will be on some issue that is of importance to you. Some examples could include improving working relations with another department, improving the quality of a customer service or improving the ways you handle difficult customers. It could be something from your home life. For me recently, one of my focuses of inquiry has been my weight. So I've been looking at what I eat, when I eat and how I could change my eating habits. I've kept a journal noting when I've been successful or not. This is a long-term inquiry for me, and it will need several cycles of inquiry to start making a difference.

Activity 1.6

8 minutes

Can you think of any focuses of inquiry that are important to you?

Comment

The key benefit of this process is that it allows you to choose your focus and make sure that it is one of significant importance to you. This focus then becomes the basis for you to design a series of cycles of inquiry with an aim of improving your professional or life practice. We will talk about this more in the final section of this book.

Now, of course, it is important to state that none of these frames is exclusive. It is very likely that as you focus on one area of learning for this module, you will notice and reflect on several critical incidents and you might well benefit from keeping a regular journal, if not daily then weekly.

Why develop your reflective skills?

Before we move on to the practice of reflective learning, I want to pause for a moment. I wonder if some of you reading this book are saying to yourselves, 'But I do this already!' We can have a sense that reflective learning is just common sense and something that we do as a natural activity during our day-to-day lives. Well, that may be true, but I would suggest that there are three important reasons for trying to develop your reflective skills beyond what you do already:

1   I would want to re-emphasise the deliberateness of reflective learning. This isn't something that is done naturally, but is something that we consciously focus on in order to improve some aspect of our lives. In undertaking reflective learning, we are deliberately seeking to change our lives and world. This is serious stuff and can be incredibly exciting!

2   Common sense can be a dangerous thing. It is rarely sensible and almost never common! Often I find that using someone else's methods helps me to notice some important point that I hadn't noticed before. The very fact that it isn't natural is what helps sensitise me to important issues and stops me being blinkered.

3   Careful reflective learning can make some of our assumptions more explicit. Have you ever noticed, when looking back on some situation that went wrong, how often the word 'assume' comes into your description? Try it and see. You might have assumed that a colleague would be at a meeting, that they would do a particular task, or that everyone would know about the report you wrote last year. It can be a crucial piece of our learning jigsaw as we make explicit the different factors that are shaping our actions. It can be quite illuminating when we stop and consider what it was that we

believed we 'didn't need to think about' because it was so obvious. Our assumptions can be a very dangerous block to learning.

We are now ready to go on to a more detailed description of three methods of reflective learning. There are many more methods, of course, and you will find some recommendations for further reading at the end of the book. The important point is not to seek out some 'correct' form of reflective learning, but to seek out a method that works for you.

2 Frameworks for reflective learning

Having introduced the ~~~~ ~~~~ ~~~~ective learning, we will now move on to look at t~~~~ ~~~~ ~~~~flecting. Frameworks can be very helpful in po~~~~ ~~~~ ~~~~hould consider and can also help us to ~~~~

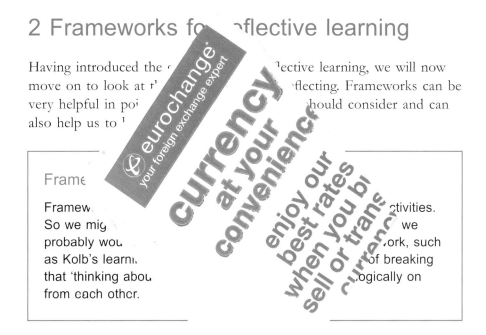

Frame~~~~

Framew~~~~
So we mig~~~~ ~~~~ctivities.
probably wou~~~~ ~~~~we
as Kolb's learni~~~~ ~~~~ork, such
that 'thinking abou~~~~ ~~~~of breaking
from each other. ~~~~ogically on

Having said that, you should stu~~~~ the frameworks below as guides rather than rules or techniques. To begin with I would recommend that you stay fairly close to one or other of these frameworks, then, as you get more experienced, try to use the parts that work for you in conjunction with elements from other reflective frameworks.

A very common visual tool for reflective frameworks is the use of a cycle or spiral. The idea is that at the end of your reflective learning you will take some action. Consequently, this action will lead to new situations for you to reflect upon and so the cycle starts again. I really want to emphasise the idea that good reflective learning involves action, trying out new ideas or testing new ways of acting. It is just too easy to think about something, come up with some good ideas and then do nothing. One way to think about this is to say that reflective learning is not a process of learning *about*; it is more a process of learning *what* and *how* to act.

Kolb's experiential learning cycle

First, we'll look at Kolb's learning cycle, which is probably the most frequently taught model of experiential, reflective learning.

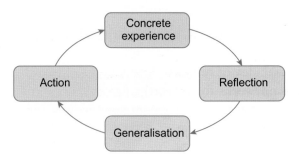

Figure 2.1 Kolb's experiential learning cycle (adapted from Kolb, 1984)

A concrete experience

If you were using Kolb's cycle, you would start with an actual experience, a sequence of events or some situation; something that you would consider a critical incident. This involves giving very careful attention to an accurate retelling of what happened, trying very hard not to edit out those elements of an event or situation that are uncomfortable to recall. When journalists are getting a story they are encouraged to answer the following questions: who, what, where, when, why and how. If you adopt this approach, the first four questions will help you sort out what happened and the final two questions will help with the next stage of reflection.

Activity 2.1

30 minutes

Go back to the event that you thought of during Activity 1.1 and use the first four questions to help you describe what happened.

Exercise 1

Who was there, who were the active participants, who said what, who was listening, who was less involved?

Comment

Do work hard to remember everyone present, even those only slightly involved. Sometimes it's easy to stop at the main 'actors'. It can be surprising just how important some people can be just by being present, and sometimes the fact that a particular person didn't do anything can be highly significant.

Exercise 2

What was the sequence of events?

Comment

Try to visualise the occasion or occasions. For example, it can be very important to notice if an event happened before or after a particular person entered a room or if it happened before or after something else was said or done. Also, be very careful in your description of what actually happened. 'Concrete experience' can be a difficult concept, as it is hard to be truly objective about what happened. We all tend to see things happening from our own perspective. So one thing you could do would be to ask someone else who was involved what they thought had happened.

Exercise 3

Where did all this happen?

Comment

At one level this is an obvious and simple question, but be careful: sometimes people can behave very differently during a conversation in a corridor than in a formal meeting in the director's office! So take time to note down where events happened and question, during your reflection, whether this was significant.

Exercise 4

When did things happen?

Comment

This can be linked to the sequence of events but it also includes times of day. For example, did your colleague get angry just because of bad work from the team or because it was the end of the day and she had had a particularly trying meeting during the afternoon?

Well, how different is your account of what happened this time? Is it more detailed? Do you think that you've added some details that might be quite important to your thinking about why things happened as they did?

Have you noticed how, with several of these questions, we have already hinted at reflecting upon the events? In part, you are already thinking through the question 'why', and this is important because your answering of that question will be much easier the more detail you include in your description of a sequence of events or situation that you are reflecting upon.

To help us understand each stage of Kolb's learning cycle, we'll look at Mary's story. As we go through the stages of Kolb's cycle I'll discuss some of the 'mental tools' that you can use to make the most of your reflective learning.

Mary's story

It was a fearful row. To be honest, Bill had suggested that I waited until the next day to talk with our Regional Manager (RM) about the loss of the McIntosh account. 'He's been in the Regional Managers' meeting all day and you know he always comes out of that drained and fed up,' Bill had said.

But I had thought it important that I got back to the agents that evening so that, perhaps, they could do something to save the situation. The RM exploded when I gave him the news, his tea mug flew across the room. 'I told you not to raise the prices!' he yelled. He was referring back to a meeting where we had discussed pricing policies for the region where McIntosh is based. I had understood his point at the time but pricing decisions are not made solely by Regional Managers like him. They also have to be okayed by the Marketing Manager and the Finance Director, and they were both very clear, when I had met with them in the FD's office, that I had to improve the margins on my accounts. At the time, I had felt that I had little option but to go for a price hike.

The RM went on and on, accusing me of disloyalty and threatening me with dismissal because of our reduced sales in the region. Denise had come in at that stage saying that she didn't think that McIntosh had left us because of the price hike. She mentioned that they had been buying less from us for some time now and wondered if the price issue was only an excuse for stopping selling our product at all. She went on to mention that she had heard rumours that McIntosh were trying to go upmarket, selling only more expensive items. This was like a red rag to a bull for the RM. 'So why didn't you know that Mary? Why do I have to hear that kind of information from Denise? She's the sales administrator for goodness sake!'

I was getting angry by now and feeling that the RM was being unfair. 'Of course Denise gets to hear more than me from the customers, she has daily conversations with them over deliveries and you have expressly instructed me to work exclusively through our agent when it comes to sales activity,' I retorted. Then we went on to discuss representative policies and local agency agreements. We argued about the quality of the agent the RM had appointed – I felt that the agent prevented me from knowing what was really going on with McIntosh. We worried over who else might be changing their product strategy and I made a strong point about the difficulty in finding new customers for low price items when we had to pay agents' commissions and restrict ourselves from doing our own customer visits. It was 7 pm before we finished and went home!

Activity 2.2

15 minutes

Go through Mary's description and note down where she answers the questions who, what, where and when.

Comment

Who: Mary, Bill, the RM, Denise, the agents, McIntosh, the Marketing Manager and Finance Director, other customers and potential customers.

What: the loss of the McIntosh account, Bill's conversation with Mary, Mary's decision that she needed to speak to the RM that afternoon, the initial explosion together with the 'mug' incident, the RM's accusations and threats, Denise's contribution, further accusations, Mary's reaction to what she sees as unfairness, the discussion continuing until 7pm.

Where: not absolutely clear, but the row seems to have happened in the sales office. There had been another meeting in the FD's office.

When: the row had happened in the later afternoon following a Regional Managers' meeting. There had also been two earlier meetings: one between Mary, the Marketing Manager and FD, and one between Mary and the RM. It is not clear when these meetings happened. There had also been some conversations between Denise and McIntosh staff, but again it is not clear when and for how long these conversations had been going on.

Did you get everyone and every detail? In particular, I wonder if you included the Marketing Manager and FD, or the existing and potential customers. None of these people were actually present at the row but their importance to what was going on is very clear. What do you think about some of the areas of doubt? Particularly interesting to me is the question about when and for how long Denise had been hearing these rumours. I think that if I were Mary, I would go and ask Denise these questions.

Reflection

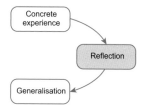

We move on now to the second stage of Kolb's learning cycle. At this stage we are interested in finding out what the really significant actions and words were and we will be answering the questions 'why' and 'how' did these things happen. We will also look at another reflective question that I find very helpful, 'so what?'

To help us work through this reflection stage we will continue to use Mary's story and see how you can look for evidence and build an understanding of what happened in the series of events that Mary is reflecting upon. Remember, the key point is not just to understand what happened but to work from that understanding towards action. I've mentioned it before but it bears repeating: reflective learning is about action!

The first task you have to do is to *frame* the issue that you are trying to deal with. As you saw earlier, framing is a process by which you put boundaries around a topic. It provides you with a way of looking at an issue. Often, as you look at an event, you can frame it in several different ways. One way that you can frame your reflection is by asking the question 'what do I want to change?' If there is nothing in need of change, then you don't have a critical incident and you really don't need to spend too much time considering things. However, the very fact that you have gone to the effort of describing a sequence of events suggests that something has gone awry or that you have a sense that those events could offer a positive area for improvement. Looking at how to frame the events Mary described will explain how to frame a reflection.

Activity 2.3

10 minutes

Take a few minutes to list the sorts of question that Mary might have been thinking about as she wrote that description of her experience with the Regional Manager.

Comment

The questions (frames) I came up with can be found in Figure 2.2 below.

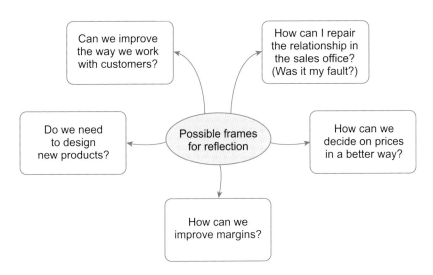

Figure 2.2 A mind map of possible frames for reflection

Any of these questions could provide a frame that would, in turn, shape Mary's reflection. Answers to the question 'why' would be very different depending on which frame she decided to use. Let's take two frames and see what evidence we come up with from Mary's description. We'll use 'How can I repair the relationship in the sales office?' and 'Can we improve the way we work with customers?' We'll make a table and use phrases from the description to remind us of relevant points.

Do you see how the important points for each way of framing the reflection are different? This is why it is vitally important that you think hard about how to frame your reflection.

Office relations	Customer relations
The RM 'drained and fed up'	Denise in daily contact with customers
'Accusing me of disloyalty'	Is the agent getting in the way?
Sales price decision mechanism	Is the agent good enough?
Denise knowing more than Mary	Cost of the agent's commission
Unfairness of RM	Complexity of pricing decisions
Appointment of agent	

Another point that you will need to consider is what timeframe to work with? For example, when looking at the office relations frame, we can see that Denise's comments caused Mary some problems in that particular row with her manager. What we don't know is whether Denise was actually trying to be helpful or if she had a history of trying to 'score points' off Mary. So Mary would have to think back to see if there were other situations when Denise tried to make things difficult, or if they have a good relationship. The concrete experience–reflection stages of Kolb's cycle are iterative. By that, I mean you may well find that, as you get underway with your reflection, you have to add to your description by thinking back or considering different events. It can be something of a snare within the critical incident method of reflection that one event can blind you to the importance of other, related events, so be careful to avoid this. Using different frames can be a help here. While you are reflecting, try to look at an event from different perspectives.

Activity 2.4

10 minutes

For the moment, we're going to look more carefully at the 'office relations' frame. How would you judge the important factors? Think about the situation as Mary describes it. What questions come to the fore? What issues would you take time to consider at greater length?

Comment

So there we have Mary reflecting upon office relations; why did a piece of bad news cause a major row? Several questions arise out of Mary's description. First, there is the simple question of whether she got the RM at a bad moment; that would probably be Bill's evaluation of the affair.

Second, it seems to me that there is an issue about pricing. From Mary's description, it seems that the RM was not involved in the final price decision for the McIntosh contract. Now that seems a slightly strange situation to me. Could it have contributed to the RM feeling that others were damaging his authority? That seems to be confirmed by his accusation that Mary is disloyal. Mary would have to work through these and other questions. For example, towards the end of Mary's account the conversation, whilst still heated, seemed to move away from personal issues and get on to important areas of policy where there are significant differences between Mary and her manager.

The many different points discussed here illustrate the importance of framing. It would be all too easy for Mary to focus on how bruised she felt and how unfairly she was treated but there seem to me to be other issues that lie below the surface of the row and they may be more important. This is a crucial aspect of the reflection stage. Don't go straight for the most obvious point but give yourself time to consider alternative causes. So far, I have focused on asking 'why' did things happen the way they did. However, you should not forget to seek answers to the question of 'how' something occurred. The important point here is to notice how a situation built up. It's very rare for there to be just one cause of any human activity and thinking through the moment-by-moment way a situation emerged can indicate other important factors that affected what happened.

Generalisation

In the third stage of Kolb's learning cycle, you will try to work out what learning you can take from your reflection and apply in other situations. The key question that you will want to answer here is 'so what?' In going through the concrete experience and reflection stages you have, in effect, revealed 'what' happened, so now you need to work out what should be the impact of those events on your future actions. You're asking 'so what?' Later you will need to ask 'now what?' I've taken these questions from Melanie Jasper's (2003) use of earlier reflective work by Borton and you might find those three questions are quite helpful to use alongside Kolb's ideas.

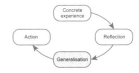

As you try to generalise aspects of your experience your goal will be to identify those aspects of a critical incident that are likely to be significant to your future actions. To do this you could ask questions under the following four headings:

- consistency

- content

- concepts

- consequences.

Let's explore each of these headings a bit, using Mary's story as an example, especially the issue of how her company manages customer relations.

Consistency

First, we can ask questions of *consistency*; things will always happen that are specific to a situation and won't apply to any other situation. For example, take Denise's contribution to Mary's row with the Regional Manager and assume that Mary and Denise are good colleagues who work well together. Considering this information, we would say that Denise's comment caused Mary problems *in that moment only* and that there is no general principle that Mary should consider for future work with Denise. However, I would suggest that the issue of the Marketing Manager and the Finance Director getting involved in pricing decisions might well be a long-term issue that Mary should consider carefully. So, the generalisation stage – sometimes called the theorising stage – is the period when you consider the longer term implications of what happened and when you try to understand where there are consistencies or patterns to certain events and trends that will affect future actions. Here are some questions that may help you:

1   Were the events ongoing or temporary? An issue here might be the involvement of the Marketing Manager and the Finance Director in pricing decisions. Was this an unfortunate, one-off event or is this a common experience?

2   Were the events central to or on the fringe of what happened? Now we want to work out whether events or situations are at the heart of what happened or just part of the surroundings. In Mary's case, the role of the agent is an example. Remember that Mary told the RM that the agent got in the way of her knowing what McIntosh were doing or wanting. Now this might just have been a quick defence that Mary put up to deflect the criticism of her not knowing about the rumours about McIntosh's change in policy or it might well be a

central complaint that had been festering for some time. If it is just a defence then the issue of agents is not likely to be a persistent one.

3   Do the events point to something that is deep or superficial? In a way this is similar to the question of centrality but asking a similar question in a different way can often be helpful to reflective learning. I would suggest that the fact that the Regional Manager was tired after a long meeting was a superficial cause of the row. Maybe Mary was unwise to talk to him then, but I suspect that apart from leaving a bad taste in the mouth it wasn't going to have a long-term effect on the department. However, the question about McIntosh changing their own selling strategy might well be very important, especially if other customers followed their example!

Content

Having asked questions about consistency, you now need to ask questions about the *content* of what happened and the people involved. Here you'll need to focus on what the events tell you about yourself, the other people involved and the problems that you are all facing.

Activity 2.5

10 minutes

So, what can you learn from Mary's story about the people involved in relations with customers? You're probably feeling a bit short of information here. Again, notice how the processes of reflection and generalisation keep sending you back to the events with further questions that will affect your description. So what would your questions be? What sort of things do you think could be important to your reflection?

Go back to Mary's story and make a list of questions.

Comment

Well, did you find that an easy task? As is so often the case with reflection, the skill is to be able to separate the significant elements from those that are of passing interest. I'll look at just two possible questions (there are always more you could ask):

1   I'm quite interested in whether the Regional Manager is under pressure. Do you notice how he has been overruled on the pricing issue? Additionally, he seems to find meetings very difficult at the moment. If he were to leave, would his policy of using agents go with him?

2   I'm interested in the agents. Are they really obstructive? Do they really block the flow of important information to Mary? How high is their commission; does it make a significant difference to the products' price?

Mary may well have the answers to these questions but, of course, there is always a problem with bias. How easy do you think that it would be for Mary to admit to herself that she might be as much of the problem as the agent? It's very difficult to be honestly critical of yourself without going overboard and always taking the blame. This is a skill that can be learned and it is an area where involving trusted friends and colleagues can help. We'll look in more detail at that in a later section.

Concepts

Two more questions will help you to theorise about what caused things to happen and generalise them into advice for the future. First, you need to look at the *concepts* that lay behind your actions. It seems that apparently daft actions often have good reasons lurking behind them! We usually have good reasons for what we do. However, what seemed a good reason at the time could be mistaken; reasoning can be built on faulty or irrelevant information or unchallenged assumptions. For example, do you think that Mary was right to speak with the Regional Manager when she did? Couldn't she have waited until the next morning? She had a sensible reason for talking with him that evening but was she wise to do so? Our actions can often be affected by 'concepts' or 'theories', commonsense, everyday theories like 'tired people can be irritable' or 'our customers are king'. It is always worth questioning the theories, assumptions or reasons that lie behind our actions.

Consequences

Second, we need to spend some time considering the *consequences* for you of what happened. These consequences largely fall into two categories: changes that you will need to make, or changes that you will need to persuade others to make. These questions take us straight into the final stage of Kolb's learning cycle, where we consider actions. But before we get there let's take a moment or two to pause.

Taking a breather!

Are you starting to get the feeling that this reflection thing is complicated? Perhaps you are wondering how anyone would get anything done if they went through all these stages every time anything happened. I wonder how many of you have thought the phrase 'analysis paralysis' as you read the last few pages. Perhaps you have thought that if you did all the analysing and thinking I've suggested, you wouldn't get anything done! There are a few points to make here:

- Yes, good reflection does take time but no, you are not going to do this kind of careful analysis for every situation. You will need to make a decision as to whether the importance of an incident merits the time to think it through carefully. It is not the practice of reflective learning that deserves time, but instead the complex situations that we have to work through that will, on occasion, merit setting some time aside to reflect upon. Our families, job and careers are important to us and if we are thoughtful, we can make a significant difference to how they prosper. Reflective learning isn't the answer to every problem but it can help.

- You do get more skilled at this and many of the questions will come to you as second nature as you get more practiced. Sometimes you'll find yourself just thinking through some of these questions as you drive somewhere or go for a walk. As you get used to reflecting on experience, you will find that it comes more easily and quickly to you.

- You will hopefully find it immensely exciting and rewarding as you gain greater influence over how you live and work!

Action

Let's get back to Kolb's reflective learning cycle. Towards the end of the generalisation stage I suggested that you consider what the consequences were for you of the events you were reflecting on. I asked you to think what you would change or what you would work towards changing.

Well, the action stage is…

…*when you get on with it!*

Don't just think about it, don't just be wise after the event, don't just grumble: get on with making a difference.

That's all there is to this stage really!

There is a little more to say, but the real message I want you to take from this section is to get on with it and take action.

There are just two questions that you need to ask yourself as you take action:

- What do I want and what do I think I can achieve?
- How will I know that I'm on the way?

THINKING OUTSIDE THE SQUARE

A few years ago, a friend of mine who worked in the logistics industry was helping me to think through a tricky work situation. I'd worked out what the important problems were and I was trying to plan what to do next. Paul asked me, 'What would "good" look like?' I found that a very helpful question. It might not be good English grammar but it helped me think through what I could realistically aim to do. More recently I have been working with a large engineering company, trying to help them improve their management of new product design and development. There were some big issues that I thought were hampering their work but I knew that these issues were under the control of the parent company. There was simply no way that I would be able to make these changes. So, I looked at areas of management where I could influence people and that's where I put my effort. I had decided what 'good' looked like.

Activity 2.6

10 minutes

Think of a tricky work or life situation that you have experienced. Can you think of how you could have applied these two questions to help guide your actions?

Comment

The crucial thing here is to think about what you are trying to achieve – about what is 'desirable'. However, it is not always possible to get everything you want, and so you might need to consider what is feasible – what's the best you can do in the circumstances? Try to be specific in setting objectives and have a clear idea of how you will know that you have been successful. Finally, especially where the learning cycle is likely to last a long time (more than two weeks, perhaps), try to pick out somc events that might indicate whether or not your objective is becoming more achievable.

My hobby is sailing dinghies. On the sails of my boat are little bits of fabric called tell-tales. One of the ways that I can know if I'm sailing well is when those tell-tales are streaming out horizontally backwards. If they start drooping down then I know that I have to adjust the tiller. Well, as you look to take action following reflection, you should try and think of what the 'tell-tales' might be for what you're planning to do. How will you know, quickly, that your action is having the desired effect? What events would encourage you that things are going well; what events might cause you to reconsider what you are doing?

So, with those two questions in mind to help guide your action, you can get on with it!

3 Alternative models for reflection

Bringing our feelings into our reflection

Kolb's learning cycle is a very rational model of how we learn. We are expected to try to be as objective as we can so that we can build up theories of why things happen. I don't know about you but I find life to be messier than that! Thoughts and behaviour aren't always rational. Now, of course, a key part of reflective learning is to help us become more thoughtful and less impulsive in our actions, but we do need to include our feelings and their effect on our actions in our reflection. The second framework that I want to introduce to you is helpful in this respect. I've taken it from a book by Mike Pedlar, John Burgoyne and Tom Boydell (2001), who are very well known for their work in helping managers to develop their skills.

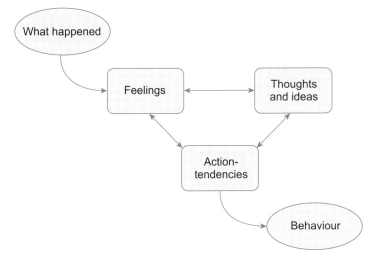

Figure 3.1 Bringing our feelings into our reflection (Pedlar et al., 2001)

This framework focuses on our response to events that happen around us. It asks us to consider why we acted as we did in particular circumstances and if there might be better ways of acting. As such, Pedlar and his colleagues recommended it as more of a long-term 'journalling' method rather than a one-off reflection on a particular event. But for now let's just look at this framework to see what it might add to our reflective skills.

There are three components involved in this reflection:

- our feelings
- our thoughts and ideas
- our action-tendencies.

As before, we'll go through them now in a little more detail:

Feelings

Especially in the West, the ability to be rational is highly prized. I won't argue with that idea here but it does have one significant negative effect. Too often we play down the importance of our emotions and feelings especially as they affect our actions. It really doesn't seem too surprising that feelings of dislike for a person, moral outrage at a course of action or fear about our ability to do a job might affect what we decide to do. We can't like everybody, sometimes other people make us angry and we wouldn't need to learn if we were confident about everything we did! So it's perfectly reasonable to expect that our feelings will affect our actions. The trouble is when, in an attempt to appear rational to ourselves and others around us, we hide those feelings and fail to take them into account.

Activity 3.1

8 minutes

Reflect back over the last week or so to any event when your think that a colleague's actions, at least in part, were shaped by his or her feelings. Can you describe the event and the actions that were displayed?

Comment

Of course, this won't have happened to you! You wouldn't let your feelings govern you at work. You have been rational and logical all the time...

... or have you?

What sort of feelings are we likely to have in a work situation? Well, the whole range. Have you ever felt:

- jealous of another person's success?
- left out of an important meeting or project?
- encouraged by your boss's praise?
- disheartened by difficulties?
- fearful of a new job?
- excited by a new project?
- intimidated by a senior colleague?

I'm sure you can add to this list; they're part of what it means to be at work or in any of life's difficult situations. They often play a significant role in how we act, so take a little time to consider them. It's not that feelings will always lead to bad actions; it's more that we need to appreciate just how we were feeling in the particular situation that we are reflecting on, in order to fully understand why we acted in the way we did.

Thoughts and ideas

The thoughts and ideas element is similar to the stages of reflection and generalisation in Kolb's learning cycle, but this time you need to think back to remember how you understood a particular situation at the time and ask questions about how you were making sense of the situation as you responded.

Jack's story

I've just been in a meeting with Chris and some of the junior engineers and I'm not happy with the way it went. Actually, if I'm honest, I'm not happy with the way I handled the situation. We're coming up to a major validation event and we're slipping behind our schedule. Chris came into our office wearing his 'I'm the Senior-Project-Manager-and-member-of-the-senior-management-team' hat. I know him when he's in that mood; he won't take no for an answer and he won't listen to any explanation longer than three words. Usually all he wants to hear is 'Yes, Chris, I'll do that right away.' It's not entirely Chris's fault, I guess that it's as much about the macho culture we have here, but it can be impossible to have a reasonable conversation.

Well, by and large, when Chris is in that sort of a mood I just keep quiet, nod my head as though I understand and use a form of words that will keep him happy but without quite committing to anything. Actually, I've become quite skilled at it! It usually works, or at least it delays the inevitable storm, but today there were three young engineers involved and one of them, Deepak, started to explain why what Chris wanted was impossible. Chris went into bulldozer mode; I sensed danger and tried to indicate to Deepak to back off. However, he went on in great engineering detail why Chris's request was impossible. I saw Chris's eyes glaze over before he gave Deepak a clear message about who was boss and exactly where Deepak was located in the company hierarchy. It was pretty unpleasant for the young man. I tried a couple of times to intervene but, if I'm honest, I knew that there was little that I could do to help. You just have to let these things blow over and then pick up the pieces.

Afterwards, I tried to talk it through with Deepak and make some sort of plan but he was very upset and angry with me for not backing him up. In the end, he stormed off. I think that he's at an interview today; we can't afford to lose him, as he's a very promising engineer. I do feel that I let him down but then I'm not sure what I could have done.

I wonder whether you have been in a similar situation. It's sadly all too common for senior managers to bully their subordinates, and it has a longer term effect than just in the moment when it happens.

Activity 3.2

5 minutes

Look back at Jack's story and see how previous experience of Chris's behaviour had shaped his thoughts on how to deal with him.

Comment

Notice how Jack's thoughts are also muddled up with his feelings. I suspect that he was feeling pretty uncomfortable during that outburst from Chris, don't you? I think most of us would feel that we wanted to help but would be uncertain of how helpful we could be. Working with other people is difficult and we need time out to reflect and see how we could do things better.

The second part of the thoughts and ideas element is to do with the ideas we had about what we could do. For Jack this centred on waiting for the storm to blow over and then picking up the pieces afterwards. It's worth noting a difference here between Kolb's learning cycle and Pedlar and his colleagues' reflective frame. When Kolb gets to the stage of thinking about action, he's talking there of what action to take next. However, when Pedlar *et al.* ask us to consider our ideas for action, they are referring to the ideas we *had* in a particular situation. The aim of the reflective learning is different. For Pedlar, Burgoyne and Boydell the reflective learning is about understanding how we behave and so giving us a greater chance to improve our performance by noticing those things in our behaviour that might have a negative effect.

Action-tendencies

Action-tendencies are those habitual ways of working that just come out of us. I tend to go for the most radical option available and am usually willing to take on people in authority for an idea that I believe in. I'm not very good at holding back and working out what is feasible and so I tend to put in a great deal of unnecessary work.

Think about your habitual types of action. In a tense situation, what do you tend to do? What is your initial response to difficult requests? Do you tend to want to analyse or get on with some action?

The answers to these questions will be your action-tendencies. Sometimes they will be helpful, but at other times they might get in the way.

Activity 3.3

8 minutes

Look back at Jack's story. What do you think that his action-tendencies were? How do you think they might have hindered Jack from taking action in this particular situation?

Comment

Jack tended to back off if Chris was in a bad mood. It appears that there is some thought behind this behaviour, but it could well be a strategy for self-preservation that had become a habit. I wonder if there was a moment in the meeting when Jack could have said to Chris, 'I think Deepak and I need to talk this through and come back to you with a plan', but his tendency toward passivity got in the way of that possibility.

Pedlar and his colleagues are offering a way for you to consider how you behave. They suggest keeping a journal over a period of time so that you can review a series of entries and spot any recurring themes. Are any feelings common? Are any thoughts and ideas consistently helpful or problematic? What are your action-tendencies, and where are they a benefit and where a hindrance? As you consider these points over a sequence of events, so you can seek to modify your behaviour. The benefit of the Pedlar reflective framework seems to be that it allows us to make explicit things that are often tacit or hidden, things like habits, feelings or ways of thinking. The way we act is often a messy affair of rational thought and less considered motivations. Try to make use of these different ideas as you seek constantly to improve your actions and performance in difficult situations.

Including others in our reflection

I think that Kolb's reflective learning cycle is a little weak in a second area. Relationships with other people can affect both what we can do and our actions. Now, you can argue that you can use the second stage of reflection to consider the actions of others but, overall, the cycle is very individualistic – it assumes that we act as independent individuals. Pedlar and his colleagues also talk a great deal about how we, as individuals behave. Anyway, neither of these two reflective frameworks explicitly emphasise how relations affect what we can achieve.

Activity 3.4

7 minutes

Look back at Jack's story. Do you think that it would make things clearer if we understood his actions as coming from interactions with Chris rather than just from considering his own feelings? What questions would you ask if you focused more on the way Jack and Chris interacted rather than on Jack's individual actions?

Comment

I wonder if it felt a little strange trying to think about a relationship as one thing. After all, we tend to think about relations as being the result of what two or more individuals do; that's why, I suspect, most reflective frameworks don't mention relations explicitly. However, if we look at the way that the two men interacted, then I think that some new questions arise. For example, why was Chris becoming aggressive? Were there any signs that Chris might not be willing to listen to long explanations? What could Jack have done to defuse a confrontation?

Do you notice that in asking these questions I am asking you to attend to the moment-by-moment way that a situation arose? This is something like the 'how' question that I introduced in the description stage of Kolb's learning cycle. What is important here is what we *attend* to in our actions.

Attend

'Attending to' is the process by which we 'look out for' or 'focus our attention upon' something. An example is when I advise managers to attend to work conversations rather than just the task in hand.

Judi Marshall (2001) has done some very helpful work in this area and we shall use some her ideas to finish this introduction to reflective learning. Marshall wrote of two attentional disciplines. First, we shall look at *inner arcs of attention*, then *outer arcs of attention* before going on to discuss how we can attend to our involvement in ongoing action. Let's look at each of these arcs of attention in a little more detail. I think that you will notice some themes coming through from earlier discussions, especially as you consider the inner arcs of attention.

Inner arcs of attention

Our inner arcs of attention focus on:

- our assumptions
- our patterns of activity
- our response to others
- the language we use
- the way we make sense of what's going on.

Marshall recommends that we attend to these inner arcs with curiosity and playfulness. This is not something to get terribly introspective about, but to notice and wonder how we could be different, to try out different assumptions or responses.

Outer arcs of attention

In attending to outer arcs we will be noticing:

- what is going on around us
- how we are affecting that
- how we are maintaining or changing a situation
- how we can test our assumptions
- how other people are making sense of the same events or situation.

Activity 3.5

10 minutes

Go back to Jack's story. Can you suggest some questions that he might ask himself if he were to use Marshall's framework to help him reflect on what happened?

Comment

I think that Jack might consider the following points:

- Was I really attending to what was going on?
- To what extent was I complicit in Chris's behaviour? To what extent was my passivity an encouragement to him being overbearing?

- More than that, in accepting the current macho-behaviour of senior management, am I actually ensuring that it continues? Is there a sense in which we all get so desensitised to aggressive behaviour that the only way that senior managers can make people aware of the importance of an issue is to become aggressive?
- How can I test my assumptions about the best way of dealing with Chris?
- Who amongst my colleagues could I talk to about this and seek ways to improve the situation?

I would suggest that these are very different to the kinds of question that were coming out of the Kolb or Pedlar *et al.* frameworks. The attentional disciplines are at their best when we learn to use them 'in the moment' rather than at some point after an event takes place. That will take quite a bit of practice, but there are two ways of getting used to them. First, you can use them alongside other reflective methods after a critical incident. Second, some time when you're in a meeting where you don't need to say much, try listening to the discussion using Marshall's inner and outer arcs of attention to frame how you notice your responses to what is going on and how other people behave.

Alongside the two attentional disciplines, Marshall proposed two further frames to help us attend to how we are involved in ongoing action. First, she wrote about consciously cycling between action and reflection. Second, she pointed out that there are times to persist, pursue and shape our world – times to be active – but there are, equally, times when we need to focus on what she calls 'communion'. These are times to focus on relationships with others, on listening and discussing. These are the cycles of inquiry I discussed earlier and the crucial thing about them is that they are active and they involve us in an ongoing inquiry. We will explore how to conduct such an inquiry in Part 2 of this book.

Part 2: 4 Introducing Productive Inquiry

Moving from reflective to productive inquiry

There are many benefits to be had from a regular reflective practice, as discussed in Part 1. There are, however, two problems that limit the usefulness of reflective learning in helping us work out what we need to do in order to make things happen. First, an emphasis on learning from experience suggests that reflective learning might be a somewhat haphazard process. It carries a sense of learning only when something significant strikes us. What if you don't have a particular experience? Will there be some learning that you don't do? Also, some people feel that reflecting on experience is only a process of retreading old ground.

A second problem with 'learning from experience' is what we mean by the word 'experience'. How do we know what experience we've just had? This problem is linked to a field within the subject of philosophy called epistemology. Now, we do not have the space within this book to tackle this subject fully, but we do need to spend a little time thinking about how confident we can be that our **account** of an experience is accurate or at least helpful to our learning.

Activity 4.1

30 minutes

Think back to a recent event that you were involved in that went wrong in some way. Perhaps it was a meeting where there was a row, perhaps it's a relationship that has gone sour, or perhaps it was a disagreement over what were the important issues in a decision that you had to take.

OK, list the people who were involved. Next, write down the story of what **you** think happened. Then, pretend that you are one or two of the other people involved and write the story again, as if **they** were telling the story. Come to think of it, it might be a really good idea, if possible, to go and ask those people for their story of what happened.

Finally, compare the stories.

Comment

I wouldn't be surprised to find that the two stories were very different, especially if you were able to get the people involved to actually tell their own story. Why is this?

Well, there are a huge number of reasons, but some obvious ones include:

- People look at events from different perspectives. For example, if I'm in a different part of a room I can probably see different events, different facial expressions or hear muttered comments that you didn't hear.
- People bring their own agenda to meetings, so something that isn't important to you (and so not worthy of noticing) may well be very important to somebody else.
- People bring different levels of pre-knowledge, so some action or word that is really significant to you may not be understood as so important to another person.

Unfortunately, it just isn't the case that one person's story of an experience is the same as another's. Consequently, the learning-from-experience that these two people will do from supposedly the same experience will be very different. The point I want to emphasise here is that learning from experience alone may not be good enough; we have to think very seriously about **how we gather the information** upon which we reflect.

So the goals of the second part of this book are to explore:

1   How we can develop a deliberate, sustained and well thought-through process by which we inquire into what actions will improve our work performance;

2   What methods of inquiry will help us gather high quality information that will help us to consider

   (a) Our working context and its demands upon our work practices

   (b) What will improve our work

   (c) How we can be sure that changes we've made have actually improved things and

   (d) How changes in our working practice will impact upon others.

In order to capture a sense of this kind of inquiry, one where the centre of our attention is how we work, our professional or social practice, I will use the term 'productive inquiry'. This is a term coined by Dewey some seventy years ago and given new life by Cook and Seeley Brown

(1999) when they argued that there was a way of knowing that centred on practice. The reason I think this term, productive inquiry, is useful is that it emphasises an idea that will become increasingly important to our inquiry: that we are 'researching' so as to make a difference. A key theme of this book, and one that I'll return to several times, is that our working practice, whether it is in paid employment or in our social life, will benefit from a practice of inquiry that isn't just about getting more information but is about changing the way we work. In a way, we will be looking at methods of inquiry that will produce new ways of working; that are productive.

Dewey's theory of inquiry

John Dewey was an American philosopher of the first half of the twentieth century. He is generally described as being a leading thinker within the Pragmatic school of psychology and philosophy. His major works centre on how we think, how we learn, how we do science and politics, and what we could do to improve our methods for doing these things. Dewey's work appears to be coming back into fashion at the moment, and certainly what he says about the practice of inquiry (Dewey, 1938) is relevant and helpful to those of us who are trying to improve the way things are done in the organisations and groups in which we are involved. We do not have time to fully explore all that Dewey had to say about his theory of inquiry but there is a key point that might help us understand and use the ideas that we will develop in the remainder of this book.

Dewey emphasised that any **inquiry is a process** in which ideas and 'facts' that are 'discovered' make a difference to the outcome of that process. That is, for Dewey, inquiry does not just *find out* things; it **changes** them.

Now, the importance to us in learning to do high quality, helpful and productive inquiry is that we will use some techniques, ideas and tools that have been developed by academic researchers who have a very different reason for their research activities. For most academic research projects, the goal is to uncover either new explanations of or insights into why things happen the way they do. The hope is, of course, that other, practical people will be able to use these explanations and insights to make things work better. You'll notice that in that last sentence I set up a divide between the academic and the practical. Not all academics would be happy with that divide and certainly Dewey would challenge it, for he argued that a logic of inquiry was at the heart of all our activities, not just scholarship. Inquiry and practice are therefore completely integrated. Inquiry is not done by some outsider trying to understand what others are doing in order to give advice about what to do next. Inquiry is done by participants who are trying to make things happen, people who are trying to produce something better.

It is this productive nature of inquiry that I want to explore with you in this book. I don't intend that readers should become academic researchers. Rather, I want to attempt to take some of the ideas and practices found in academic research methods and re-imagine them into practices that can help people in the thick of organisational life, where we work with others, in both formal and informal contexts, to make things happen.

Centring practice rather than knowledge through inquiry

So a key point that will affect much of what I write and how you read and work with my writing is that we're interested in organisational practice; how we work, co-ordinate and make things happen within organisations. Academic research, on the other hand, is generally more interested in developing theory, knowledge and explanation of what is going on. The logic is that by understanding the underlying and important characteristics of organisational life, we can build theories. Now, that theory and knowledge may well be very important to organisational participants and certainly much of the material presented in academic courses of learning draws on the findings and conclusions of such research. However, the demands made of academic researchers in constructing robust theory are different from the demands placed on organisational participants who are asked to 'make things happen'.

As a consequence, we will need to look carefully at how academic researchers go about research. We will then consider which of these disciplines and practices will be helpful and which will be inappropriate to those of us who are more concerned with getting on with organisational work and making things happen. I do not want to spend too long getting entwined in esoteric, academic debates, but if we want to use ideas from academic research intelligently within our own practice-centred inquiries, then we do need to be aware of some important terms and debates.

Three important features of a productive inquiry

Before we go on to explore the details and methods of an inquiry into our organisational practice, there are three important features of such an inquiry that will affect how we undertake one.

Inquiry is always social

There is absolutely no way that you can do a productive inquiry on your own. Even if your inquiry is designed by yourself, for the benefit of your career or so that you can do your own job better, it will always involve other people.

Activity 4.2

15 minutes

Think of some action (either one that you will need to take in the next week or so or one that you have taken recently). Note down who you think will be affected by your actions, who you will need to involve in making sure that the action is successful, and whose support and agreement you'll need.

Comment

In a recent project, I wanted to run some planning workshops with a group of engineers from a large company. I had designed the workshop and would facilitate it but I still needed the involvement of some colleagues to help with the running of the day. I was conscious that some of the engineers who would be working with me were also involved in activities run by another colleague in a different department. From earlier experience, I also knew that I wouldn't get any of the engineers along to the workshop if I hadn't first got the approval of their Chief Programme Engineer.

Before I could put a workshop date into my diary, I had to go around all these different people to ask their opinions and ensure their support and active involvement. A practice-centred inquiry will always lead to action, and that action will always affect others. It's crucial that before you take action, you think through and ask what the impact of your action will be on others.

Let's look at each of those three social aspects of inquiry in a little more detail.

Implications for others

Any action we take will affect others. For example, if you have a hedge in your garden, then you might well consider not trimming it every year. Now, there's a good and a bad reason for that! But let's work on the basis that you're not simply trying to avoid some hard work but that you've heard that less trimmed hedges provide better homes for birds. OK, so your inquiry is about whether not trimming the hedge every year increases the number of birds in your garden. The hedge grows … and that has an impact on your neighbours; it might well reduce the amount of sunlight they get. I'm sure that you could think of other examples for yourself; say, having a party in a block of flats or deciding to come to work late when you're working flexi-time.

An important issue in any action or practice-centred inquiry is that there will probably be consequences to your action that will affect people in unintended ways. You need to think through who those people might be and inquire into their likely response to the change.

Co-ordinating with others

If we were to take the example of the party in the block of flats, one option might be to check with the neighbours upstairs when they'll be out (so that they're not inconvenienced by the noise of extra cars parking). For work-based inquiries, you may well need to draw on the collaboration of colleagues. Whose help will be needed? Who might be required to do some work prior to our own intended action?

Support from others

Another feature of an inquiry's social nature is that an inquirer will often require support from others. I mentioned above that sometimes we actually need to collaborate with colleagues and friends, but there are other, perhaps more passive, forms of support. In a way, sometimes we need to know that even if they won't actually help us, people won't get in the way! Examples of this might be when we want to try out a new idea at work. It might well be worthwhile checking with your boss that she's OK with the idea. That isn't always possible, or even wise, but you do need to consider the following issues:

- Are there people who could obstruct what you're doing?
- If you are trying out a new way of working, might a colleague have to pick up some extra work? For example, your inquiry might mean that you're out of the office more frequently, so your colleague has to answer the phone more often. Will they be OK with that?

- What if the inquiry goes wrong? Even the best-laid plans and ideas go wrong sometimes. What does the downside of your inquiry look like? What could go wrong and do the people who might be affected know and support the plan? Or, if they don't know, will you at least be able to cover your tracks in case of problems?

I'm conscious that, in raising these issues, I'm possibly painting a negative picture of inquiry. I really don't want to do that and I would want to emphasise that, in a later chapter, we will look at ways of increasing the chances that any inquiry you put into action will succeed. However, the fact of the matter is that in any inquiry, others are involved both helpfully and less helpfully, and you will need to take this important point on board as you plan yours.

Inquiry is transitory

A vital point to consider as you undertake a practice-centred inquiry is that you are not looking for eternal truth, but for an insight into **what to do next** or what course of action to take in the long term. This point is important for two reasons. First, it should encourage you to get on with an inquiry and not wait until you've got everything perfectly organised. As I've mentioned above, there are issues that you need to be careful about, but care can be taken *as* you get on with an inquiry. Many of the ideas in this book are taken from the academic area of research methods. For very good reasons, books and articles in this area emphasise a rigorous following of methods and prescriptions. For many researchers this is vitally important because they are seeking to test out theories or explore new ideas, and their intention is to produce robust research reports that others can rely upon. If others are going to base their policies, actions and research careers on your writing, then you'd better be ultra-careful to get things right. Of course, for professional practitioners working in areas such as medicine, or any area where the safety of others is concerned, a similar level of rigour will be required in designing an inquiry. However, for most of us and for most of the time, we will be able to put right problems we cause during any inquiry into our practice.

You never step into the same river twice, situations change and action that was appropriate then might not be so helpful now. An ancient Greek philosopher, Heraclitus, argued that all of life was a flow; we could never step into the same river twice. The water in the river had changed and so had we. Whilst our experience would tell us that some things do tend to stay the same or at least appear to stay the same, still we are surrounded by the transitoriness of life. For example, we think of a really good thing to say just a moment too late and the chance has gone, or we phone a friend to encourage them before an interview, only to find that they've just left. A few years ago there was a series of advertisements for a mobile phone network saying that life was made up of 'one-to-ones', and there is an insight in that. We could rephrase it slightly and say that life is lived moment by moment.

Now what is the point of all this, rather esoteric, philosophising? Well, just this: a practice-centred inquiry, in contrast to knowledge output research, is concerned with action. And the way that we can act is always, to some extent, dependent upon circumstances at a particular moment. A few examples might help me explain this.

- Imagine that you and I have been involved in a long-running argument about some issue. I phone you up to encourage you just before you attend a totally separate but difficult meeting. However, you immediately start on the topic of our disagreement and the moment has gone.

- Last autumn I was on the Greek island of Naxos. I was sitting having a drink with my brother and his wife with a beautiful sunset in front of us. As I looked out across the sea, there was a moment when a fishing boat was caught beautifully in the sun's rays. I reached for my camera but by the time I was sorted, the boat had moved on and the photograph was lost.

- Recently, I wanted to discuss with a colleague an issue about a module that we were working on. By the time we finally met, the situation had changed and we didn't need to discuss the course but she had just received news of a research project so our conversation took a different turn – very useful but different from my plan.

Activity 4.3

10 minutes

Recall one or two recent examples of how your actions were affected by a situation. Think through how that situation either restricted your choice of action or perhaps opened up more opportunities than you had previously thought possible.

Comment

Later in this book we will look at some research work by Marshall (1999; 2001; 2004) that has examined how an action researcher can explore the effect that on-going relations can have on the possibilities for taking action.

There is a very real tension here for the practice-centred, participant inquirer to handle. On the one hand, pausing for a moment while we gather more information may well be the best action; and yet that pause might mean that we miss the one moment when it is possible to act.

Inquiry involves a continual testing and retesting of emerging sensemaking

So why have I taken some time with the last few points about the social and transitory nature of a practice-centred inquiry? Essentially, my point is this: that inquiry is a process of making sense of how your own actions fit within an ongoing and ever-changing set of relations. On the one hand, this makes a practice-centred inquiry very difficult though not impossible; on the other, it carries some benefits as long as we take care to focus our attention on what we should do next. There are three steps involved in this 'taking care to focus our attention':

1 Accept that we will not have perfect information:

   (a) We won't know everything there is to know about a situation.

   (b) Consequently, we will not be able to be sure of the relative importance of different factors.

   (c) Some of the things that we may 'know' about any situation are likely to be tacit, that is, we are unaware that we know anything.

   Consequently, we may need to be cautious in asserting that we know 'what's going on around here' and equally careful about our actions.

2 Take care to attend to what evidence we do have and constantly ask two questions:

   (a) What further information would help and how easily obtainable is it?

   (b) How can I act in a way that 'gets on with it' but is sensitive to the uncertainty that may require us to change tack?

These are issues of judgement that will come with practice. A crucial point here is not to get stuck waiting for perfect information before acting. Some of the discussion in Chapter 8 may help here.

3   Constantly test our emerging sensemaking about our actions in relation to the work context:

(a) **Testing by asking questions** – who might have more or better information on a given situation? Who might have a different perspective? Who might think differently from us and so challenge 'truths' that we take for granted?

(b) **Testing by taking action** – at its simplest, if we take action based on faulty or incomplete information things may well not turn out as we hoped. Surprisingly, they sometimes go better than we had hoped! However, the question remains: how can we act in a manner that gives an emerging situation time to evolve? How can we act in such a way that any possible problems can be addressed without calamity?

One other thing is worth mentioning here. We have already come across a central feature of any practice-centred inquiry that will help us handle its transitory nature, and that is the **cycle of inquiry**, where we take time to act and then reflect upon that action. We shall return later to the role of cycles of inquiry in developing high quality inquiry but for now, I just want to flag up two points. First, a practice-centred inquiry is an emerging process, not a once-and-for-all action that discovers the truth. Second, it is a process where imperfect action is taken, but where a constant attention to the evidence that comes to light within the cycles of action and reflection can be immensely helpful in improving our work practice within our professional or social life.

What's involved in a productive inquiry?

Before we move on to discuss questions of 'how' we go about conducting a productive inquiry, I want to pause and take a look at the overall process and then focus on one stage that is crucial, but which is easily overlooked.

An overview of a productive inquiry

Figure 4.1 is a diagram that I will use again in Chapter 8, where I will use it to help me break down the different stages that we go through to make sense of any information that we have gathered. Here, I want us to look at the process as a whole.

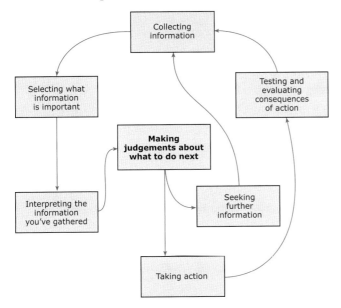

Figure 4.1 A process of productive inquiry

Let me re-emphasise a key point here. The ultimate goal of a productive inquiry is to take action that we can then evaluate and test as to whether it is beneficial to our work practice. All the different techniques that I'll be introducing are aimed at helping you develop skills of inquiry that will enable you to improve your work practice.

Now, at the heart of the diagram is the stage of **making judgements**. As I will say again in Chapter 8, there is a way in which this stage will permeate the whole process of inquiry. You will constantly find yourself making judgements, for example:

- Should I speak with this person today?
- Do I trust that source of information?
- Have I got enough information?
- What's the best way of gathering information at this moment?

We'll be revisiting all of these questions, and more, in the following chapters, but I want now to discuss one judgement that will have a significant effect on the quality of your inquiry. Before you start, and then at several moments during your inquiry, you will need to consider what you are focusing on.

Developing a focus for your productive inquiry

Academic researchers often talk about the importance of a 'research question'. By that we mean that we need to be sure of the question we're answering, for the somewhat obvious reason that it'll help us know what information will answer that question and when we have actually found an answer! It sounds so obvious, doesn't it? But you would be surprised how often we find it difficult to keep focusing on one particular research question. I don't fully know why; perhaps it's because things change, our interests change or some piece of information just changes our whole perspective.

In the same way, if you and I are interested in undertaking a productive inquiry that will change the way we work, then we will need to keep revisiting the focus of our inquiry. Why is this? Well, it relates to those three important features of productive inquiry that I discussed above:

- Inquiry is always social

- Inquiry is transitory

- Inquiry involves a continual testing and retesting of emerging sensemaking.

Each of these three features will mean that the focus of your inquiry will need revision and refinement.

Activity 4.4

5 minutes

Before we go any further, jot down a series of possible focuses of inquiry that would make sense within your workplace.

Comment

Some of the focuses of inquiry that I and students I've worked with have used include:

- An engineer who was fed up with losing arguments with accountants and so set up an inquiry to learn how to 'beat them at their own game'!

- A social care worker who couldn't understand why there was always conflict with the health care workers they were supposedly collaborating with.

- A warehouse supervisor who wanted the great ideas from review meetings to be put into action rather than just forgotten about.

- A local shopkeeper who wanted to find a way of organising people in the village to help each other and work together on projects.

So, how can we go about developing a helpful focus to our inquiry? Figure 4.2 might be helpful in this.

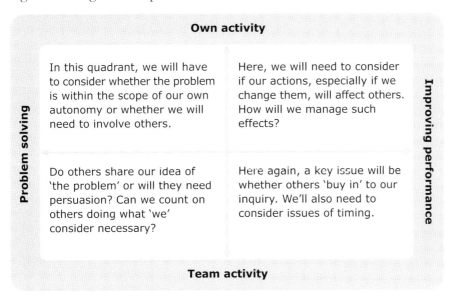

Own activity

In this quadrant, we will have to consider whether the problem is within the scope of our own autonomy or whether we will need to involve others.

Here, we will need to consider if our actions, especially if we change them, will affect others. How will we manage such effects?

Do others share our idea of 'the problem' or will they need persuasion? Can we count on others doing what 'we' consider necessary?

Here again, a key issue will be whether others 'buy in' to our inquiry. We'll also need to consider issues of timing.

Problem solving

Improving performance

Team activity

Figure 4.2 Things to consider when choosing the focus of an inquiry

The diagram is created by asking a couple of questions that will help us consider our inquiry focus. First, is our inquiry going to be centred on **our own** activity or on **a team's** activity? This will have implications as to how much work we need to do in building a shared view of what needs to be done. If we want to change the way a group or team of people work, then we're going to need to gain their support.

A second question asks whether our inquiry's aim is to improve our work performance or to solve a particular work problem. Now, this question isn't nearly so neat and clearly defined as the first question. In the end, you might well find that in order to solve a particular work problem you need to improve your own work performance. OK, so this is not a science; you are not aiming for a precise definition here. Rather, you are just trying to get a feel for what the focus in your inquiry is. If you find yourself in any doubt, then ask someone you trust (perhaps a mentor) for advice.

So, let's put those questions together and see what the implications might be for your inquiry.

You'll see that in each quadrant, slightly different questions emerge as important. What is common throughout the figure is the importance of 'contracting' with others. These 'others' might include colleagues, bosses, friends or clients, and they will play an important part in your inquiry. Indeed, we might find that the process of getting a group of people involved is a part of the inquiry. We may well find that we need to gather information that will persuade people. I'll tackle this point again when I explore what might be meant by 'testing for plausibility' in the next chapter.

Summary

In this chapter, I have introduced you to the idea of conducting a productive inquiry with a view to improving your work and social practice. In doing this I have contrasted the practice of **productive inquiry** with reflective learning and academic research. I haven't done this to say that either reflective learning or academic research is inferior. Rather, I have merely wanted to emphasise the importance of two things about doing a productive inquiry. First, productive inquiry is a **deliberate, thorough process** of gathering information. Second, productive inquiry is not satisfied with the gathering of information but is centred on **taking action**. In the light of these important factors, we can now explore **how** we can conduct a productive inquiry.

5 Building an overview of your productive inquiry

Aims of this chapter

In the previous chapter I introduced the concept of **productive inquiry**, which I proposed as a way of deliberately and persistently seeking to improve our work practice, whether that work be in formal paid employment or in less formal, social situations. In order to outline some important themes of a productive inquiry, I contrasted it with:

- learning from experience, for I wanted to emphasise the deliberate and sustained quality of a productive inquiry; and

- academic research, for I wanted to emphasise that a productive inquiry is centred on developing our work practice rather than constructing new knowledge.

Now, I want to explore with you **how we go about** a productive inquiry. This will take four chapters. In later chapters I will introduce you to specific techniques used by researchers for gathering information and we will discuss some methods that will help us make sense of the information that we have gathered. But before we get into some of the details of how to undertake a productive inquiry, I want us to take a step back and build up our understanding of the reasoning behind some of the techniques that we will use later. In order to do this, we will explore three topics.

First,   we will split our thinking about work practice into three issues, so that we can get a more focused view on the sort of questions that we will be asking during a productive inquiry.

Second,   we will consider some specific questions that we might well be asking about our work practice and see how asking different questions will lead to us using different inquiry methods.

Third,   I will introduce you to three major research traditions that will form the bedrock of the methods that we will learn about in later chapters.

Introduction

I mentioned in the previous chapter that many of the ideas in this part of the book are taken from the academic discipline of research methodology. Additionally, I mentioned that one reason I use the term 'productive inquiry' is so that I can emphasise the importance of action as the outcome of inquiry in contrast to the academic researcher's ambition to generate knowledge. These two ideas should not be seen as contradictory; indeed, at times you may well see yourself needing to gain knowledge about a situation before action. The point to be made here is one of emphasis. What is important for an organisational participant is a question of what action to take, and often it is possible to act entirely successfully on faulty information.

Why am I emphasising this point? Well, as you read some materials about research methods, and especially if you read other research methods books, you will find that academic researchers take great care in developing accurate, or at least rich, accounts of their research subject. For academics the search for accuracy or depth of insight is often more important than time constraints. This will rarely be the case for managers or other organisational participants. You are going to have to find ways of managing a tension between the need for high quality information and time constraints.

So what methods are available to you for inquiry and how can you choose when to use them? Crucially, we need to go back to the question of what you are seeking information for; this will help you decide what information you need at particular stages of the inquiry. Categorising some of the different areas of inquiry might help you think this through.

Areas of inquiry

When you are considering any action you will need to gather information within three areas:

- mapping the terrain
- testing for plausibility
- evaluating performance.

Mapping the terrain

A while ago, I was asked by a social care manager to help her with a problem that was emerging in her department. Essentially, there appeared to be a growing conflict between her team and a health care team that they were working with. My first job in this short project was to get some idea about what was going on. I had my friend's story about the problem but I wanted to hear how the other participants described what was happening.

On another occasion, I was asked to help a company develop better relations with its suppliers. The company's managers knew there was a problem and thought that it lay with its suppliers and some unhelpful attitudes. Again, I started by trying to find out what the different parties to the problem were saying about the situation. As I listened to the suppliers speak, I didn't think that they were unco-operative but something one of them said got me looking at the computerised order system and that, in turn, made me notice the whole mechanism that my employing company used for stock control.

More recently, I was involved in some youth work in my village. There had been quite a lot of angry accusations flying around in the preceding months and our first job seemed to be to get hold of some hard evidence of how many problems there had been, how many young people had been involved, what exactly had happened and who else was willing to lend a hand.

In each of the above three stories, before I could take any action that might be helpful I had to 'get into' the situation – find out what was really going on or understand the concerns of people involved. I had to appreciate the context within which I would be working and taking action.

Activity 5.1

5 minutes

Look again at the three short stories I told and note down how I was gathering different kinds of information about my inquiry contexts.

Comment

Each story was a little different with different demands. In the final story, I really wanted to get some of the facts of what had happened, while in the second case I found that the real problem was different from the initially suggested cause of difficulties, so I had to change my investigation and follow a trail of activities until I found where there was a breakdown in communication. In the first story, I was thrown into a tricky meeting where I was able, by being an outsider, to ask people to tell their stories so that I could attend to the different perspectives in the room. I was then able to make some suggestions for how they could collaborate better.

Mark Fenton-O'Creevy remembers the following story of an inquiry that he was involved in. Notice how in his inquiry he started to build up more insight into some of the important relations within the organisation he was working with. It's probably also worth linking this story to the point I made in the previous chapter about the importance of 'contracting' with important 'others' who might be involved in your inquiry. You'll see how some important characters in Mark's inquiry had very different ideas about what his research would be about!

Mark Fenton-O'Creevy, professor of Organisation Studies at the OU Business School, says:

'I was commissioned by a large company to carry out and advise on the results of an employee attitude survey. I designed a questionnaire on the basis of focus groups with staff and interviews with the senior management team. To ensure the senior team members were fully committed to the process and to acting on the results, they were interviewed and later asked to comment on a draft questionnaire. The HR director and the chief executive (CE) of a particular division made extensive and repeated attempts to change the wording of questions and the issues focused on.

'Both seemed to have conflicting agendas. The divisional CE was particularly aggressive in his attempts to influence the nature of the survey. During an extended interview with me it became clear that he perceived the survey as part of a campaign by the HR director to undermine his position. He had achieved considerable cost savings in his part of the business. The HR director believed this to have been at the expense of very damaging reductions in staff morale and trust in the management team. Consequently, the HR director was keen to focus on staff morale, trust and perceived style of senior management communication. The divisional CE wished the survey (if it happened at all) to focus on staff perceptions of cost management and business performance.'

Mark had found himself in a tricky situation. Sometimes, I'm afraid, inquiry that is likely to involve changes can have important political implications and these may well have to be managed within the inquiry itself. Sometimes it's just not possible to prepare for every eventuality! But Mark's inquiry into the working context quickly alerted him to relationships that might well have affected how he conducted the rest of his inquiry.

Recognising what needs action

I would suggest that when you start any productive inquiry, your first consideration will be what is going on that needs some change and consequently a deliberate, thorough inquiry. I suspect that you will already have one or two areas of your social or professional work in mind at this stage, so the issue you have to consider is: what lines of inquiry should I follow? There's no way of creating a full list of every possible line of inquiry but here are four questions you can ask that may help you think this through:

- What are other people's attitudes and opinions?

  It is quite possible that an issue that you see as a problem is not recognised as such by others. Alternatively, you may find that other people's perspectives are really helpful to you in working out what you are thinking and planning to do. You will find that I'll be repeating these points in the next section, where I discuss how we can test your ideas for plausibility, so you might be able to do two things at the same time here.

- What is the real problem?

  As in my short stories above, I often find that my initial ideas about a problem get refined as I follow a trail of activity or ask others' opinions. There are times when I have to 'dig around a bit' to work out what is **really** 'going on around here'.

- What are the important details?

  It may sound trivial, but sometimes it is very important to check your facts. Recently, I was involved in a project and a colleague's name was mentioned as a possible collaborator. I had my doubts; the person had a reputation for not delivering their work on time and I thought that they had been slow with some work for me. I checked up and found that I was incorrect. Their work had been done on time. You do need to check up on relevant details: what are the actual sales figures? What was the attendance at that meeting? Who did say what?

- What am I able to affect?

  This is a tricky point, and it's easy to be either too optimistic or pessimistic. So make a point of checking with colleagues, bosses and friends what you will be able to have an effect on.

Activity 5.2

5–10 minutes

Think about some area of your work where you might consider undertaking a productive inquiry. What sort of details do you think might be important to get right?

Comment

This is one of those exercises that could either be very quick or go on for ever! A couple of questions might help you here. On one hand, if you think you don't need to check up on particular details, ask yourself if these are 'facts' that everyone knows or if, maybe, there might be an **assumption** in your understanding. In any case, it might be worth a quick check on the details. On the other hand, it is quite possible to fear that you can't go on until you've confirmed every detail. In this case, the helpful question to ask is: how important is this information to what I do next?

Testing for plausibility

Once you have identified a need for action, you will then enter a phase where you are considering what action to take. As you consider a possible course of action you will need to test out whether it is likely to work well. If you have time, or if the cost of the action is so great that the cost of inquiry merits it, then it is often possible to use mathematical and accounting modelling systems to help you predict the outcome of different courses of action. Such processes will generally, however, be beyond the scope of the day-to-day practice of our work. Still, you need to check out if your ideas for new courses of action are plausible. There are several areas of inquiry here:

- Will key people support your course of action?
  - Does your course of action fit with what they value highly?
  - Might your course of action help them achieve their own goals or obstruct them?

- ○ Will you make demands on people that they might not be able to fulfil?
  - ○ There are likely to be other important questions like the above that are specific to your own situation.
- Are there any other activities going on that will obstruct or at least affect your course of action?
- Do people you respect agree with your intended action?
- Is there any information about the particular work context that could make you think again?

Activity 5.3

10 minutes

Think of an action that you are likely to take within the next day or so (at work or in your social life). Who is it likely to affect? How might you check up on how they might be affected and how might you test their support?

Comment

Let's take a simple example of changing the date of a meeting. There are some obvious questions that you'll need to consider.

- Can other meeting participants make the new date and time?
- How urgent might other participants consider the meeting? Some might be relaxed about a delay whilst, for others, that same delay might be really problematic.
- Might the new meeting time mean that either an important or a difficult person won't be able to come? Is this good or bad news?!

Now, this is pretty straightforward stuff and you might not consider it worthwhile for an entire book to be devoted to inquiry methods just to find out if you can change a meeting. Well, of course this was a trivial example to illustrate a point. However, a couple of the above questions hit on some subtle information about colleagues' values and interests, and inquiring into these factors might well need considerable care.

Evaluating performance

As you take action you will need to evaluate the success, or otherwise, of your action. So you will ask yourself a whole range of questions, for example:

- Is there any hard evidence of the benefits and costs of your actions?
- Have colleagues 'bought into' your ideas?
- Are you sensing, noticing or able to record any evidence that you are making positive progress in your practice?

You will notice in this short list of questions (and they're by no means the only questions you could ask) that they will create a mix of answers, some of which are clear and others that are very vague and unspecific. As we go through the next three chapters you will find that we will explore ways by which you can handle the complexity of these various kinds of information. For the moment, however, an important point to make is that, in a productive inquiry, you will need to be sensitive to a wide array of evidence that may well not give you an absolutely reliable answer. Instead, you may find that inquiry material will increase or decrease your confidence in the action you are taking. This process, which I will call sensemaking, is a tricky but vital part of any practice-centred inquiry.

Definition: Sensemaking

This term is very common amongst qualitative researchers and actually means much the same as the more common term 'making sense of' events, comments and so on.

Before we go on to investigate different methods of inquiry, there are a couple more points to make about evaluating performance. I've emphasised that a key issue in a practice-centred inquiry is that it involves taking action. Unfortunately, it takes time for the consequences of those actions to become obvious. Furthermore, many actions that we take will have very equivocal consequences. By that I mean that an action could have very good consequences for one group of people whilst others might suffer. Obviously, in such circumstances you will get a very different evaluation of the success of any action depending upon your perspective and who you ask! So in evaluating your work and social practice you will have to be aware of three limitations to your inquiry.

First, however careful you are, your understanding or sensemaking about a situation will always be **partial**. You will never have the whole picture. Second, your sensemaking will always involve **judgements**, the weighing up of contradictory evidence. Finally, you need to develop ways of picking up evidence as you go along in the inquiry, so rather than a pursuit of truth, inquiry is often an ongoing **process of sensemaking**. You will constantly be looking to pick up hints. As you might recall from Chapter 2, I tend to think of this as being like my hobby of sailing, where little bits of wool on the sail, called tell-tales, indicate whether I'm sailing well. They don't tell me if I'm sailing to the right place but they can help me to sail fast and close to the best course.

'Brainstorm is working on trying to discover the shopaholic gene.'

Quantitative and qualitative approaches to research

Research (or inquiry as we will call it from now on) is commonly split into two categories: quantitative and qualitative research. This is not always a helpful divide but we'll use it for the moment to help us consider some important questions that might help you shape your inquiry. Quantitative research involves careful measuring, perhaps through surveys or questionnaires or perhaps through undertaking carefully controlled experiments. The goal of quantitative research is to get as accurate a view of 'the big picture' as possible. Most quantitative researchers are aware that they aren't able to be 100 per cent sure that what they're concluding is absolutely accurate, but they do believe that if they use the right research methods well, they will get the best possible picture of a situation.

Qualitative researchers, on the other hand, point out that surveys and experiments are rather blunt instruments for exploring the everyday 'hows' and 'whys' of social and working life. Instead, they use a series of methods for interacting with people so as to build a story of what is going on. By and large, qualitative researchers accept that this attention to detail means that they can't 'paint the big picture', but they argue that their detailed stories of how people are interacting and thinking are crucially important to our understanding of organisational life.

The academic debate between quantitative and qualitative researchers is ongoing and will almost certainly never be resolved (thus giving academics the promise of many happy hours thinking and writing about these matters. Well, it does keep us off the street!). For some researchers the debate touches on very deeply held values and beliefs, while for others it is a practical issue of which approach is best suited to answering the kinds of questions that are being asked.

From an organisational practice perspective, the crucial issue for organisational participants is what sort of questions our work context is asking (see Figure 5.1). In seeking to work out what to do next, we need to decide whether we are asking large-scale questions such as:

- Is there a market need for this new product?
- Will the majority of our worldwide staff benefit from this new incentive scheme?
- Will the local population accept our factory producing new chemicals or testing products on animals?

If you were to ask these questions of a few people then you would be unlikely to be confident that their answers reliably reflected the whole population of the market, company or town. As a result, answers to these large-scale questions need some very careful design and safeguards to ensure that the information gathered is valid and reliable.

Ingredients:

Holika Holika Pig Clear Black Head 3-step Kit (1step) Water, Hamamelis Virginiana (Witch Hazel) Water, Butylene Glycol, Sodium Lauroyl Sarcosinate, Salvia Officinalis (Sage) Leaf Extract, Viscum Album (Mistletoe) Extract, Juniperus Communis Fruit Extract, Arctium Majus Root Extract, Mentha Piperita (Peppermint) Leaf Extract, Caprylyl Glycol, Saponaria Officinalis Root Extract, Hypericum Perforatum Extract, 1,2-Hexanediol, Propanediol, Illicium Verum (Anise) Fruit Extract, CitrusMedicaLimonum(Lemon)FruitExtract, Chrysanthemum Indicum Flower Extract, Camellia Sinensis Leaf Extract, Melissa Officinalis Leaf Extract, RosmarinusOfficinalis (Rosemary)LeafExtract, Aspalathus Linearis Leaf Extract, ThymusVulgaris(Thyme)Flower/LeafExtract, Jasminum Officinale (Jasmine) Extract, Vaccinium Myrtillus Fruit/Leaf Extract, Saccharum Officinarum (Sugar Cane) Extract, Acer Saccharum (Sugar Maple) Extract, CitrusAurantiumDulcis(Orange)FruitExtract, Aloe Barbadensis Leaf Juice, Fragrance(Parfum)

Holika Holika Pig Clear Black Head 3-step Kit (2step) Water, PVP, Dimethicone Copolyol, Kaolin, Titanium Dioxide, VP/VA Copolymer, Propylene Glycol, Methylparaben, Citrus Limon (Lemon) Fruit Extract, CI 17200

Holika Holika Pig Clear Black Head 3-step Kit (3step) Water, Glycerin, Propanediol, Sodium Hyaluronate, Hydroxyethylcellulose, PEG-60 Hydrogenated Castor Oil, Erythritol, Trehalose, Caprylyl Glycol, 1,2-Hexanediol, Disodium EDTA, Dipotassium Glycyrrhizate, Illicium Verum (Anise) Fruit Extract, CitrusMedicaLimonum (Lemon) FruitExtract, Diospyros Kaki Leaf Extract, Citrus Aurantifolia (Lime) Fruit Extract, Aloe Barbadensis Leaf Juice, Vitis Vinifera (Grape) Fruit Extract, Chlorphenesin, Phenoxyethanol, Fragrance(Parfum)

Holika Holika 🦋

Holika Holika – *Pig Nose* Clear Blackhead 3 step kit

Okay, so the name *Pig Nose* may not be the most appealing for a beauty product, but this product has a stellar reputation in Korea for being highly effective in blackhead reduction and removal.

This is a 3-steps kit perfect for pore control. The first step opens your pores which allows for blackhead removal. The second step removes blackheads and the third step minimizes skin pores.

Directions

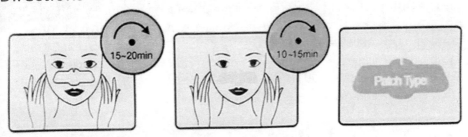

1- Thoroughly cleanse and pat dry face.
2- Place **Step-1** sheet on nose for 15-20 minutes.
3- Remove slowly and wipe away any blackheads or impurities from pores.
4- Wet the nose with water and place **Step-2** strip on nose tightly.
5- After 10-15 minutes, the strip should be completely dry. Slowly remove, starting at an edge.
6- Place **Step-3** gel sheet on nose.
7- Remove after 10-15 minutes and gently tap the nose to help absorption of residue gel.
8- **Top tip** – Some people like to put **Step- 3** in the fridge before use.
9- Use 1-2 weekly as skin condition improves.

As with any skincare product, if your skin reacts in any uncomfortable way, remove the mask and wash face with cool water.

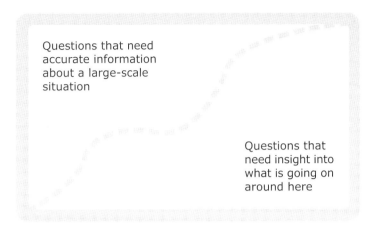

Questions that need accurate information about a large-scale situation

Questions that need insight into what is going on around here

Figure 5.1 Deciding on a quantitative or qualitative approach

Researcher's experience: Jon Billsberry, a senior lecturer at the Open University Business School, suggests another benefit of using quantitative or survey research methods.

'To me, surveys are just ways of having interviews with larger numbers of people. Just like interviews I have to construct my questions carefully and think about the sort of information I need. Sometimes this is quantitative and sometimes qualitative. Both can work well in questionnaires. The real benefit from surveys is the added power they give me in helping to convince people. Interview data can always be viewed suspiciously by people as it so obviously involves individual interpretation of meaning, whereas the (usually) more systemic approach of a survey and the ability to say with some confidence that "75% of people would prefer a …" rather than "three people told me that …" makes them a valuable weapon in the leaders' armoury.'

Another point to make here is that these questions also tend to be centred on some pretty big questions that will be linked to major organisational decisions. There are many times, however, when such research methods would get in the way of important organisational action. Finding the answer to these questions will take time and often managers need to act quickly; just as importantly, sometimes the information gathered from these large-scale questions offers a general view of what people are thinking rather than the detailed ideas about a particular group or team of people that a manager might need. In these cases, the apparent accuracy of a survey will actually be illusory and we will need a different set of research methods that give greater attention to the details and, if we're honest, messy unpredictability of organisational life.

This is where qualitative research methods become important. Qualitative methods don't try to give you a quantified and statistical picture of the 'whole situation', but rather they will help you gather information that gives you *insight* into a situation. So, for organisational participants, the important question at this moment is captured in Figure 5.1: do you need information that gives you an accurate picture of the **whole situation** or do you need information that will give you insight into a **particular situation**?

Upon the answer to this question will rest your choice of qualitative or quantitative research methods. From the point of view of this book, we will be focusing on organisational situations where information is needed quickly so that action can be taken in day-to-day organisational settings, so we'll be focusing on qualitative methods and one in particular called action research. I'll be outlining the details of these methods in more detail in later chapters.

Activity 5.4

10 minutes

Take some time to consider the sort of activities that you're involved in day by day or the sort of projects that you have to be involved in from time to time. By and large, is the information that you need to get on and do your job more about detailed insight or the overall picture?

Comment

Let me look at my own work as an example. I'm undertaking a project about creating courses for work-based learning at post-graduate level. So here I do need some information about the overall market picture. What sort of learning, training and development will companies and other organisations pay for? I also need to have some information about some of the institutions of the professionals involved (such as nurses, engineers and HR managers). Finally, I will need to judge what sort of qualifications and structures will suit colleagues in different faculties at the Open University. So, for this project, I will need to ask both the large-scale, overall questions as well as the detailed, insight-seeking questions. I would say that it is very unusual for me to be thinking of using quantitative research methods. Usually, even when I was in marketing, I found that the cost (in terms of time and money) far outweighed the likely benefits.

'So in other words, we're hoping to discover what makes the nitty, gritty.'

A further consideration is important for practitioner-inquirers and that is a judgement of the cost of inquiry, both in terms of cash and time in relation to the value of the information that is to be gathered. Of course, if you have no money available then that does restrict your choices, but it may be that you do have the time to undertake a serious quantitative or qualitative inquiry. A key point here is to remember that the most important issue in a practice-centred inquiry is when you will next need to take action. To consider this we need to think about a central building block of practice-centred inquiries, the **cycle of inquiry**. This is an idea that arose out of one of the traditions of research to which we will now turn.

Traditions of research that inform productive inquiry

In preparing this book I have drawn upon three different traditions of research methodology: action research, ethnography and grounded theory. Let's explore each one in turn and see how they contribute to our own practice of productive inquiry.

Action research: cycles of inquiry

Any practice-centred inquiry will be built upon a series of cycles of inquiry where action will create a need to reflect upon the consequences of that action and the reflection will, in turn, lead to further action.

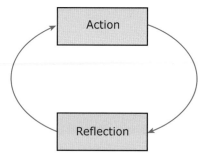

Figure 5.2 The cycle of inquiry

Depending on the circumstances, the timing of those cycles of inquiry will be longer or shorter. In some circumstances, you will be required to act almost immediately, to the point where there is hardly any time to reflect at all. On other occasions, for example if you're looking at how you run a monthly meeting, you'll have a month to ask questions, gather information and reflect on how you might do things differently next time. The amount of inquiry that you can do will depend on the length of this cycle of inquiry.

Activity 5.5

5–15 minutes

Consider the following examples of practice-centred inquiry and estimate what length the likely cycle of inquiry will be.

(a) A manager seeking to improve sales performance (she reports to the board quarterly but customers tend to buy on a fortnightly basis).

(b) A stock controller working in a busy warehouse, who is seeking to reduce stockholding costs (the stock of goods with a high unit value tends to move slowly, whilst other stock is of lower value but moves in greater volume and faster).

(c) An engineer working with component testing software doing virtual quality tests.

Comment

There aren't right answers here. Maybe the manager would check sales with each quarterly report or on a fortnightly basis, depending on how consistent sales are over the period – but there again, inconsistency might be just the information that the manager is looking for! The stock controller might have different cycles of inquiry for different products and the engineer might well be able to do several cycles of inquiry on her computer before lunch!

In each case the length of the cycle of inquiry will depend on a series of factors. Go back to the list and work out what you think might be the important factors for each case. I won't give you the right answers for there are none, but I'll just make the point that one of the major benefits of working in cycles of inquiry is that they give you considerable flexibility to change aspects of your inquiry (such as the timing) for further cycles.

Cycles of inquiry play another two important roles within a productive inquiry. First, they provide moments when you can assess how an inquiry is going and change or develop the actions you are taking. An example of this can be found in Nolan's (2005) account of his own inquiry. Patrick Nolan was a businessman who had known both deprivation and business success. He sought to bring these two aspects of his life together in a project that brought government, industry and the population of a deprived town together to provide information and training so as to help those people gain long-term employment. At one stage Nolan writes:

> In some situations I felt it was like being in a choir and singing out of tune. With my business friends I could easily empathize with their desire for substantial investment in a large project for quick results; on the other hand my Ballymun colleague argued for a more modest initiation, ground in the local communities and earning credibility in incremental fashion. I could equally agree with that view. I then began to realise that at these meetings I was at one point seeing the world, and especially the issue at hand,

through the business or corporate lens, and at another point, I was viewing it through the lens of the Ballymun reality. They were two very different views ... this key insight of the marriage of the differing lenses was to be of continuing relevance in the evolution of the [project].

(Source: Nolan, 2005, p. 306)

For Nolan, the problem was to get very different people to collaborate and it must have been easy at times to think that these two groups were being difficult or foolish. However, as he chaired the meetings, his reflections offered him a different insight that shaped how he carried on with that project.

Activity 5.6

15 minutes

Think of some project or task that you're involved in, socially or in employment, where things have got a bit stuck. Mull over why you think that is the case and then write it down. Now, note down what evidence you have for coming to that conclusion.

Comment

For Nolan, the evidence was more about his own sense of 'belonging' to the two different groups. He wrote, 'I personified the experience' of both the local community and the businessmen. Sometimes the evidence we work on in practice-centred inquiry is that 'inner sense'. At other times we have firmer evidence: things people have said or written, statistics, or the actions we have seen people take. An important point for this book is that, by and large, it's a good idea to check the evidence for these 'inner senses'.

Second, cycles of inquiry provide the opportunity for trying out new ideas. There are three points here:

1   Cycles of inquiry give you a chance to test out the practicality of new ideas in 'real time'. This enables you to assess the impact of these ideas: are they beneficial or not? Additionally, you may well get the chance to see if implementing your new ideas will have any unintended consequences.

2   But they also provide some boundaries around your initiatives. Taking an initiative and making changes within organisational practice can be a daunting affair. It might well be that you are uncertain about the benefits of your new idea and so need to try it out in a reasonably safe place. Using cycles of inquiry can help you to scope your inquiry and so, if necessary, gain the support of significant other participants who might be affected by your initiative.

3   Finally, you are not only trying out the new ideas but also testing their value. In doing this you will need to design a cycle of inquiry with an eye to how you will evaluate the outcome. We'll deal with this in much more detail in Chapter 8.

You will find that we discuss cycles of inquiry frequently throughout this book and each time we do we'll add another layer to the richness of our understanding of the process and, hopefully, help to build up our capacity to undertake meaningful and helpful inquiries into our practice.

There are two other major research traditions that I will draw on in the writing of the next three chapters – ethnographic research methods and grounded theory – so I'll introduce them to you briefly now.

Ethnographic research methods

I would locate all the methods that I discuss in the following two chapters as working within an overall ethnographic research perspective. Not all researchers would agree with that classification and if you explore research methods further, you'll find that the topics I cover in the following chapters can also be found in writing about

- qualitative research
- secondary, documentary and archival research
- case study research
- grounded theory.

So why am I locating these within one tradition? Well, basically because I'm assuming that most of the people reading this book will be conducting their inquiry within the context of their own work or social life. I doubt that many of you will be heading out into a totally new work context. Why is that important? I think that it's important because ethnography is a research methodology that emphasises how things happen, how people relate and how people make sense of their lives; it involves the researcher becoming close enough to their research situation to understand a particular situation as an *insider*.

A little bit about ethnography's history might help you to understand this point. Ethnographic research gained popularity in the early twentieth century amongst the western anthropologists who were trying to understand the social activities of communities very different from their own. One of the problems that they noticed was that, if they weren't careful, their research findings said as much about their own assumptions, prejudices and societal norms as they said about the particular community they were researching. Consequently, they devised research methods that helped them move from being naïve 'outsiders' to being competent 'insiders'. They were trying to learn the ways of the community from the inside rather than as detached and objective observers.

Now, I would suggest that in conducting a productive inquiry, you will be doing much that an ethnographer would do, in terms of seeking to 'get under the skin' of your own work context, whether it is in a formal organisation or in your social life. The one difference might be that you will probably already be an active member of the work context which you choose for your productive inquiry. This can be a benefit or a disadvantage, as David Coghlan discusses in his article 'Insider action research projects', which you can find as a reading at the end of this book. The point that I would make is that as you read these different inquiry methods, think of them not so much as methods for gathering information as methods for 'getting under the skin' of the working context where you are attempting to make things happen.

Grounded theory

Grounded theory was developed in the 1960s by Barney Glaser and Anselm Strauss (Glaser and Strauss, 1967). It was one of a number of research methods that emerged at that time as social scientists started to look for new ways of doing social sciences. Up until that point, social research had largely been done by academics who had developed hypotheses to explain the social world and then conducted research to test those hypotheses and so develop a theory of what was going on. Glaser and Strauss started from the other end, so to speak. They sought to gather data about what was going on and then gradually build theories grounded in the data that they were gathering.

In an ideal investigation, Glaser and Strauss argued, a researcher would start with no theories, no assumptions and no prejudices. They would gather all kinds of data from interviews and observations and from that data they would start to build their theories. They would then conduct a further round of investigations to test that theory and refine and develop it until they reached a point that they called 'theoretical saturation'. They would then propose a theory to explain what was going on in the particular context that they had been investigating.

In the forty or more years since the publication of *The Discovery of Grounded Theory,* there have been many developments of the practice of grounded theory and many of the ideas Glaser and Strauss developed have made their way into other research methodologies. Strauss himself came to question some of his original ideas; for example, he came to doubt if a researcher could ever approach an investigation without any pre-judgements or assumptions. For a productive inquirer involved in action researching their own practice in a work context, what is particularly helpful in grounded theory are some of the techniques that Glaser and Strauss developed to test and re-investigate their emerging theorising of what was going on. I will use many of these ideas to help us make sense of the information that we have gathered during our inquiry.

Summary

In this chapter we have identified three phases of inquiry. These three phases are:

- mapping the terrain
- testing for plausibility
- evaluating performance.

Whilst our objectives will change between these three phases, it is very possible that we will use similar methods in each. As we undertake each phase we will need to consider what sort of information will be helpful to our inquiry.

This question then leads on to the second point we covered in this chapter, for we looked at the difference of focus involved in using either quantitative or qualitative methods of inquiry. Whilst each of these groups of methods has genuine benefits, I suggested that for the purposes of this book we would be concentrating on qualitative methods. This was for two reasons: first, quantitative methods require very much more time to do well than qualitative methods; and second, most of our day-to-day practice happens at a level of detail and fast-moving complexity that suit qualitative methods.

Finally, I introduced you to three major research traditions that will form the basis of the rest of this book. These were ethnography, grounded theory and, perhaps most importantly, action research.

We'll now move on to look at particular methods that you might find helpful within your inquiry.

6 Methods of inquiry: conversations and interviews

<table>
<tr><td>

Note

Having given you an overview of the major research traditions that we will be using in this part of the book, we now move on to the key methods that you will find helpful in a productive inquiry. You may well find that you need to read this and the following chapter twice. So read them quickly the first time and then read the subsequent chapter on 'Making sense of your information', before returning to these two chapters on inquiry methods. It may be that you find some of the suggestions in the following sections make more sense as they are linked to the process of interpreting, evaluating and acting upon information that you gather.

</td></tr>
</table>

Aims of this chapter

In the previous chapter I introduced you to the important research traditions that underlie productive inquiry. Now we turn our attention to learning about, and so developing, skills in using particular inquiry methods. There are many ways of distinguishing between different methods of gathering information. Look at any book on research methods and it'll have some subtle differences from another, so there is no right way to approach this subject. We shall explore inquiry methods under two headings:

- Asking questions
- Documents (including statistics), artefacts and observation.

In this chapter we'll concentrate on asking people questions and in the next we'll discuss briefly the role of statistics and records. We will then spend longer exploring the potential of observation, documents and physical objects (artefacts) to help us make sense of our work context and actions.

Asking questions

At the heart of any inquiry is the activity of asking questions. In this section, I want us to think through the various ways that we can do this. I shall split it into different types:

1 Interviews

2 Conversations.

Definition: Respondent

For ease of writing, I will tend to use another unusual term in writing about interviews. A **respondent** is a person who is asked questions and whose answers are considered by an inquirer. It is significant that I have used this term rather than, say, informant or interviewee. The significance will become more apparent as we explore the different types of interviews and conversations you might undertake in your inquiry. Not all questions are answered by information – sometimes you will get opinions or feelings – and not all conversations are formal interviews with an interviewee, and so I'll use the one term respondent to capture all the people that you'll talk to during your inquiry.

How questions shape answers

So why do I split asking questions into these two types? Well, in answering that question I shall first deal with some crucial issues about the process of gathering information from other people. You see, the way you ask your questions will have a significant effect on the answers you're given. They will be affected by the context, the words you use and your tone.

The context affects the answer

A couple of examples will help make sense of this. First, imagine that you ask a senior colleague about a complex issue on her way to a meeting, for which she is already late. Do you think that she'll give the same answer as if you asked her the same question when she's winding down at the end of the week? Second, you want to ask a question about your firm's marketing strategy and its impact on operations; do you think you'd get a fair answer from the manufacturing director shortly after he's had a furious row with the sales and marketing director?

Now these examples are somewhat extreme, but they do illustrate the problem of choosing the best context to get answers that will help you develop successful practice. So how can you make a wise decision about where and when to ask someone your questions? Here are five questions that might help you decide.

1 **Do you have many or only a few (perhaps one) questions to ask?**

This is a simple point; if you only have one quick question to ask then obviously it won't be necessary to organise a formal interview. Just seek an appropriate moment to ask your question. If, however, you have a series of related questions then this will probably need a fixed period of time when you won't be interrupted.

2 **Does your question require a considered or spontaneous answer?**

Some questions will require your respondent to think carefully; perhaps you are asking her to make a judgement or evaluate some piece of information. On the other hand, sometimes you will want a spontaneous answer, one that hasn't been thought about for too long. Of course, you have to be careful with questions of the latter sort; are you being fair to your respondent in not giving them time to think?

3 **Does your respondent have time available for an extended conversation or would they appreciate a very brief conversation?**

Before now, I have got halfway through a series of questions with a colleague when I noticed them looking at their watch and displaying an increasing desire to be somewhere else. Such a situation does not bode well for the quality of the answers that you'll get!

4 **Is the answer to your question likely to be of a sensitive or confidential nature?**

An extreme example of this would be 'What do you think of Joe's chance of promotion?', just as Joe was standing next to you. Do you think that the answer might be affected by Joe's presence?

5 **What is your relationship with the respondent?**

Are you asking a question of a friend, your boss, a stranger or a subordinate? Each is likely to answer your question differently. Your friend might well try to think what answer would help you. An older, more senior colleague might shape her answer so as to give you advice or she might dismiss the question with a cursory answer.

A subordinate might want to please you or be worried about how their answer might affect them.

'What I'm about to tell you is extremely confidential, Ravenhurst ... I want you to promise me that you'll keep it under your hat.'

Each of these questions will help you consider how your respondent's answers might be affected by the context in which you talk with them. As you think those issues through you will then work out the best way to tackle the conversation with your respondent. Of course, there are times when you can't organise events in the best possible way and you will have to be satisfied with a less than perfect 'interview'. There are two points to consider when this happens. First, it becomes really important in such situations to keep a good record of what happened and what you think might have affected the answer you were given (I'll say more about keeping field notes in Chapters 7 and 8). Second, as you make sense of what your respondent has said, you will need to consider how the context affected his or her answer. (I'll write more about this in the section 'Reflexivity' in Chapter 8, for it is a very important aspect of the process of making sense of or interpreting what you hear. This is also illustrated in what I write in the next few sections.)

Your words will affect the answer

How you ask your questions will have an effect on the answers given.

Activity 6.1

5 minutes

Take a look at Box 6.1, which is a scene from the 1980s satire, *Yes, Prime Minister.*

Comment

Notice how the nature of the questions Sir Humphrey asks pushes Bernard towards the final answer that he wants. These are called leading questions. Also notice how the questions require a simple yes or no answer; these are called closed questions.

Box 6.1	
Sir Humphrey	You know what happens: nice young lady comes up to you. Obviously you want to create a good impression, you don't want to look a fool, do you? So she starts asking you some questions: Mr. Woolley, are you worried about the number of young people without jobs?
Bernard	Yes.
Sir H.	Are you worried about the rise in crime among teenagers?
Bernard	Yes.
Sir H.	Do you think there is a lack of discipline in our Comprehensive schools?
Bernard	Yes.
Sir H.	Do you think young people welcome some authority and leadership in their lives?
Bernard	Yes.
Sir H.	Do you think they respond to a challenge?
Bernard	Yes.

Sir H.	Would you be in favour of reintroducing National Service?
Bernard	Oh ... well, I suppose I might be.
Sir H.	Yes or no?
Bernard	Yes.
Sir H.	Of course you would, Bernard. After all you've been told you can't say no to that. So they don't mention the first five questions and they publish the last one.
Bernard	Is that really what they do?
Sir H.	Well, not the reputable ones, no, but there aren't many of those. So alternatively the young lady can get the opposite result.
Bernard	How?
Sir H.	Mr. Woolley, are you worried about the danger of war?
Bernard	Yes.
Sir H.	Are you worried about the growth of armaments?
Bernard	Yes.
Sir H.	Do you think there is a danger in giving young people guns and teaching them how to kill?
Bernard	Yes.
Sir H.	Do you think it is wrong to force people to take up arms against their will?
Bernard	Yes.
Sir H.	Would you oppose the reintroduction of National Service?
Bernard	Yes.
Sir H.	There you are, you see, Bernard. The perfect balanced sample.

(Source: *Yes, Prime Minister,* 1986)

Now, as a general piece of advice, you should avoid asking leading questions unless, like Sir Humphrey, you want to make a point and so get something done. Even then, it's probably unwise and it certainly is likely to provide you with information of a very doubtful quality. Closed questions can also be problematic. There are some occasions, especially in questionnaires and surveys, where closed questions are necessary; for example, you might want to know if a colleague was at a particular meeting. However, in a practice-centred inquiry, you are often looking for information from people you will be working with and open questions give a respondent more opportunity to shape the answers she gives. There may be a benefit in this as it will give you a deeper sense of how this colleague will co-ordinate with you as you take action. I'll say more about this aspect of asking questions in the section on interviews below. The point I want to make here, however, is that the way you ask questions will shape the answers you get and you will need to think very carefully about your questions, either before you ask them or later as you try to make sense of the answers.

Your tone will affect the answer

In addition to the particular words you use, your tone of voice will affect the answers that you are given.

Activity 6.2

5 minutes

Consider the following question: 'You wouldn't argue with the boss, would you?' This same question could be asked in very different tones of voice, for example:

- In a threatening voice by a senior manager
- In a voice of 'wide-eyed' shock and awe
- In a matter-of-fact voice by a market researcher.

What do you think the answer would be to each tone of voice?

Comment

Here again the relationship between the questioner and respondent is crucial to how the question is understood by the respondent. I suspect that you can identify somewhat different answers to the same question!

When good enough is better than perfect

So, how can you handle these complications? (To be honest, I've only touched on some of the ways in which we can affect the answers our respondents give us.) It is tempting to think that we must aim for some sort of perfection in our interviewing techniques and, indeed, some books on research methods appear to aim for that goal. In a practice-centred inquiry, however, perfect interview technique is less important than getting timely and relevant information. So, for example, waiting a week for the perfect context for a formal interview with a senior colleague might well mean that important and urgent action is delayed unhelpfully. There is a real possibility that aspiring for the 'perfect' will obstruct you in achieving a 'good enough' result. I'll say more about how to achieve good quality inquiry later, but for now, as you undertake a practice-centred inquiry, you will need to judge whether the upside of getting quick information is worth the downside of that information being flawed. This is one of those areas where keeping good field notes is vital, for you can record your sense that a colleague's comment might have been influenced by the way you asked the question. I shall write more about field notes in Chapter 8.

Interviews

Let's first consider those times when you will set up an interview, in contrast to those times when you grab a quick word with a colleague and ask them an important question. For in looking at these more formal interviews, we can see how you might deal with some of the 'problems' that we've identified above and then, later, we can see if we can use any of these ideas to help with the informal, chance conversations that are likely to be an important part of any practice-centred inquiry.

The four stages of an interview

An interview is likely to go through four stages:

1 Introduction	In this stage you need to explain what the topic of the interview is and possibly why you are conducting the interview with that particular person. You have to be careful at this stage that your introduction doesn't give too much of a steer to your respondent. Imagine starting off an interview with the sentence, 'I want to find out what's going wrong with the students and how badly the books are affecting them.' Well, that introduction has probably stopped a series of other topics from being discussed. So your introduction has to be carefully thought about. It needs to be clear enough to interest your respondent but be careful that it does not become leading, in suggesting the kind of answers that you want.
2 The schedule	All interviews will have some sort of schedule of questions. As I suggest below, there are differences in how detailed that schedule will be. Sometimes you'll have a carefully worded list of questions. On other occasions you'll have only a list of general topics you want to discuss.
3 A summary	It's often a good idea at the end of the interview to summarise what you have learned from it; indeed, you might do this on a couple of occasions during the interview as well. At such points you outline what you have understood to have been said. This will give your respondent the opportunity to correct any misunderstandings.
4 The end	This may sound trivial, but do end by thanking your respondent for giving you their time, and do make sure that you end on time. If you have said that the interview will only take fifteen minutes or half an hour, then be ready to end at that time. I have often found that once they get onto a topic, people will give you more time, even when they are very busy; but you must never presume upon that and you must be sensitive to the need to end an interview at the convenience of your respondent.

Types of interview

A common way to look at interviewing people is to distinguish between structured, semi-structured and unstructured interviews. None of them is *best* and none of them is without problems, so your decision on how to design an interview will always be a matter of judgement. We'll think about how you make that judgement in a moment, but first we'll describe each interview in a little more detail. I would want to stress, however, that there are not three, *distinct* types of interview: structured, unstructured or semi-structured. Rather, these different types of interview are on a continuum (see Figure 6.1) and you will find yourself making quite fine judgements as to whether you want to be *more* structured or *less* structured in your interviewing technique.

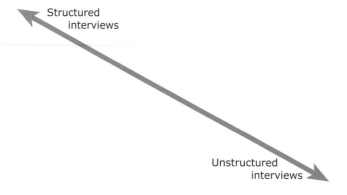

Structured
interviews

Unstructured
interviews

Figure 6.1 The interview continuum

Structured interviews

In a structured interview you will have a set schedule of questions from which you will not deviate. Indeed, at the most structured end of this type of interview, you will detail the very wording of each question. So for a structured interview you will go through several stages of preparation:

1 Work out an overview of what sort of information you want to gather and who you will be interviewing.

2 Design the questions that you will want to ask, taking care to make your wording clear so that it can't be misunderstood. You'll also try to be careful to ask questions that are sensitive to your interviewees.

3 Work out the best and most logical order for your questions. You want to avoid jumping from one topic to another during an interview. If you have several questions on the same, similar or

related topics, then put them together as that will help your respondent to think through the topic or remember details of an incident.

4 Pilot your question schedule, looking for questions that puzzle your respondents, lead to digressions or cause you any difficulties.

There are several benefits to preparing and piloting structured interviews in this way:

- This level of preparation may well help you word your questions sensitively …

- … and will help you ensure that you don't ask leading questions and that you avoid any bias in your questions.

- As you undertake a couple of pilot interviews you will get a very clear indication of how successful the interviews will be. This will help you adjust and improve the wording and order of your questions, giving you a better chance of conducting a consistent and good set of interviews.

Researcher's experience: Jon Billsberry gives this important advice from his experience of conducting interviews.

'One thing I always try to do is to pilot my questionnaires. I do this in two ways. First, I ask a few people to complete it to tell me if the questions make sense, whether there are any spelling mistakes, and to check the instructions. I guess everyone does this. But I do a second check as well. I imagine that fifty or so people have completed the questionnaire and I put numbers and words into my spreadsheet to mimic what the results could look like. I then imagine that I am writing up my report and try to incorporate data. As I do this, it makes me think about what the questions are really asking and what conclusions I can draw from them. It also tells me what sort of analysis I can do. I do this because in my early years as a researcher I found that I got people to complete my surveys and then found errors and problems that defied analysis.'

Unstructured interviews

At the opposite end of the structure continuum are completely unstructured interviews.

Jim had a meeting with the big cheese.

So how do you go about an unstructured interview? Well, I've found that there are two elements of a successful interview. First, you have to provide a **hook;** a theme or topic that interests your respondent. I have bad memories of times when I tried to interview someone about a topic that bored them! This hook has to be specific enough for the respondent to recognise its importance and its relevance to them. So, for example, it's unlikely that a sales manager would understand why she's being interviewed about the details of factory policy, but she might have something to say about how factory efficiency affects her sales success. Similarly, details of how a hospital recruits cleaning staff might not be very important to a consultant surgeon, but I bet that she'll consider the cleanliness of the wards and operating theatres to be very important. You therefore need to choose your respondents carefully so that they'll have something to say about a topic you're interested in, and then you'll have to describe that topic in a way that hooks your respondent into the interview. This might mean that you word the introduction to your interview slightly differently for each respondent.

Researcher's experience: Caroline Ramsey explains why she tends to use completely unstructured interviews.

'I guess that when I'm working with organisations, my particular interest is in finding out how people talk in that organisation, what sort of things are important to them and how they distinguish good from bad or successful from unsuccessful. So I'm possibly less interested in the topic they are actually talking about and more interested in their manner of talk. As a consequence, I want my respondents to choose what they talk about and how they talk about it. Unstructured interviews, often involving me asking managers to tell me stories of important incidents, are really helpful as I try to co-ordinate with members of an organisation.'

Second, you'll need to establish a **rhythm** to your interview. I use the term rhythm to capture the sense in which unstructured interviews are different from structured interviews. In a structured interview, you will have a carefully planned and organised schedule of questions. That won't be the case in unstructured interviews, but you will need some method of encouraging your respondent to talk and of helping them focus on the main theme of the interview. How can you do this without a set sequence of questions? Here are three possible rhythms that you might use. They are only examples and you might find that you develop one of your own that fits better with your own working context. Having introduced the general theme of the interview:

- Ask what the key issues are, or what have been the significant events. Then ask for **stories** that illustrate that issue or event.

- Ask how your respondent would evaluate the current situation or past events, or what they think will happen. Here you are asking for their **opinions**.

- Or you could ask about their **feelings** about how a situation or project is progressing.

In each case, you are asking open questions that seek to encourage your respondent to talk freely, with as little direction from you as possible.

Definition: Open and closed questions

You can ask questions that have one right answer. For example, you could ask if it rained on Tuesday. The answer is either yes or no. Similarly, in asking: 'What was our sales volume in August?', you will expect one answer. These are **closed** questions. On the other hand, you might ask if the rain is likely to be heavy enough on Tuesday to stop us going jogging or you could ask the sales manager why sales had fallen during August. These questions would be **open** questions because they do not have a correct answer; rather they will elicit a more free-flowing response.

Semi-structured

As the name implies, a semi-structured interview has some of the characteristics of both the structured and unstructured interview. There is no one correct way of doing this; it is an issue of judgement. Having taken a decision to conduct a semi-structured interview, you will plan an overall structure for it. Almost certainly you will either have a list of topics that you want to cover or a list of questions that are important. The more experienced you become at interviewing, the more you will tend to work to a list of topics; but when you first conduct an interview, it might be wisest to work out the best way of asking specific questions.

Where a semi-structured interview differs from a more structured conversation is in the way you give space to your respondent to expand on a particular topic. To do this you will tend to ask open rather than closed questions. If all your questions are purely about facts and details, you won't get much further than a list of those details. If, on the other hand, you ask questions that offer your respondent more scope to discuss something that interests them, you are likely to get richer data.

Activity 6.3

15 minutes

Write answers to the following two questions.

1   What subjects have you covered in your Open University studies so far?

2   What are the most significant things that you've learned during your Open University studies so far?

Which of these questions took longer to answer and which answer do you think would tell me more about you as a person, student and professional?

Comment

I have little doubt that your answer to the second question will have been much longer and that, whilst your answer to the first may have been quite a long list of topics from the different modules that you have studied, your answer to the second will almost certainly tell me which subjects have been more interesting to you, relevant to your professional work and influential in what you consider important.

On the other hand, your answers to the first question may be immensely helpful to me as I work out where to go in an interview. As has so often been the case in our discussion of inquiry, it isn't a case of what is right and what is wrong; more, it is a case of working out whether open or closed questions are useful at a particular moment in an inquiry.

Take another look at question 2 in Activity 6.3. What do you think was the most important word in that question? I think that there are two really important words that make all the difference to how you answered the second question. They are

- 'learned'

- 'significant'.

In shifting from 'subjects you have covered' to 'what you've learned', I have opened up a much wider space for you to explore as you reply to my question. For example, you might well have learned about business topics such as marketing or finance but you have also learned about how well you can study on your own. Perhaps, given that this module is unlikely to have been your first one, you've also learned that 'I can do it! I can study at university!' For many people starting off their learning, the fact that they can do it when they had always thought that learning was beyond them is the biggest thing they learn.

> **Researcher's experience:** Mark Fenton-O'Creevy tells an interesting story.
>
> 'My first degree was in pure mathematics and I learned a great deal about linear analysis, topological spaces and other esoteric subjects. However, I also learned problems come well-defined and neatly packaged and that there are clear-cut, right or wrong answers. As I've done more work in the field of management, I've had to 'unlearn' much of my learning from my first degree! Often diagnosing the problem is the hard part and most answers are partial or at best "good enough".'

Not all learning is always helpful learning, as Mark points out. In changing my question from 'subjects you've covered' to 'learning', I've offered space for more personal, subjective details to inform an answer.

The second important word that I've used is 'significant'. First, this word asks the respondent to evaluate their learning. I'm not just asking for a list of topics now; I'm asking for your judgement as to what is making a difference, what is becoming important to you. So perhaps you answered my second question by writing: 'The most significant thing I've learned about business is the importance of people.' I wouldn't be surprised if something like that has featured in many answers, but it begs a set of other questions, doesn't it? How have you learned that? Why is it important? What are the implications for you of the learning? Can you give any examples of 'the importance of people' in your own working life? These are called **supplementary questions** and they are crucial to building up a successful semi- or unstructured interview.

How do you know which type of interview to use?

In Table 6.1 I have summarised the main benefits of and problems with the different types of interview. As I've mentioned before there isn't a right way of interviewing and you will find yourself choosing to question people in a more or less structured manner; it won't always be a case of one or the other style. Anyway, here are some brief outlines of why you might choose one of the three types.

Table 6.1 Benefits of and problems with different types of interview

Interview Type	Benefits	Problems
Structured	• helps keep a consistency when you are interviewing several different people about the same issue • can be used to contrast responses from people in different groups • questions can be designed before an interview, so that your wording can be made clear • you can pilot your questions beforehand, so that you can see if they work • whilst more care, and time, is needed in setting these interviews up, making sense of what's been said is easier	• structure gets in the way of an organic interview; does not enable you to change your questions in tune with an emerging conversation, or follow up interesting themes, issues or inconsistencies • structures the interview from your perspective rather than the respondent's
Unstructured	• gives more scope for the respondent to 'structure' the interview • gives more opportunity for issues that are new to you to be discussed • allows you to get a feel for how your respondent might work with your proposed changes • gives more opportunity to explore apparent inconsistencies, either within the interview itself or with information you have gathered from other sources	• interviews can go off the topic you want to discuss • interpreting the interview can often be time consuming • perhaps easier for experienced interviewers
Semi-structured	• can give some of the benefits of both structured and unstructured • possibly a good compromise for those new to conducting interviews	• semi-structured interviews won't save you either from being too restrictive in your questions or from respondents who ignore your concerns and talk about their own issues!

Reasons that you might choose to conduct a more structured interview

If you've never conducted an interview before, you might well want to have your questions set out in front of you so that you don't forget an important question. In addition to settling your nerves it might also help you plan the questions and word them in a way that doesn't confuse people. Asking questions is a skilled job and it does take time to build your confidence; experience will help you feel at ease in reading interview situations and asking good questions with less preparation. So be prepared to learn on the job, so to speak. It might well be worth practising with friends, especially if you're about to interview your boss. And that point makes me think that maybe you should be careful about who to interview first!

There are other important reasons for asking your questions in a more structured way. For example, if you want to compare perceptions across different groups of people then you need to make sure that you ask them exactly the same questions. This will ensure that any differences are due to differences in the people you asked, not variation in your questions. In the same way, the more important it is that you build up a 'true' picture of a situation, the more important it is that you ask all your respondents the same questions. Consequently the quality of the questions becomes more important which, in turn, will mean that you need to prepare those questions more carefully.

Structured interviews are not without their problems. For example, they restrict your potential for following up an interesting point made by your respondent. Additionally, they can restrict your flexibility to change direction in an interview should that become necessary. Following a fixed set of questions can also make it very difficult to create a sense of conversation that may help to open up interesting themes of inquiry.

Reasons you might choose to conduct a less structured interview

There are three major reasons behind the choice of unstructured interview methods. First, an unstructured interview gives you far greater flexibility to follow themes that emerge during the interview. There are occasions when your respondent says something that is really interesting which you want to follow up with supplementary questions. A second reason for conducting unstructured interviews is that they give greater scope for the respondents to set the agenda for what is discussed. Obviously, the interviewer will have an overview of the general topic to be discussed, but there are always several perspectives from which a topic can be viewed. On occasions it can be important to let the respondent, rather than the interviewer, set that perspective for the discussion. This is because you may very well want to see how different people approach the same general topic; those differences are part of your inquiry.

A final reason for using a more unstructured approach is particular to a practice-centred inquiry. Often in conducting an interview you will not only be seeking out information but will also want to get a feel for how your respondent will co-ordinate with your intended new way of working. In such circumstances, giving space for your respondent to set an agenda will enable you to hear more of what is important to them and so attune your future actions to their values and opinions. Additionally, unstructured interviews give you, as the interviewer, greater scope to change your questions and inputs in tune with an emerging conversation. So you can test your new ideas or respond to a challenge or encouragement.

The problems with unstructured interviews include the danger of your respondents heading off into irrelevant topics. There is also a problem that as an unstructured interview goes on, it can be very difficult to fit in a particular question that you want to ask. Indeed, on occasions, I have got so interested in what my respondent was telling me that I forgot to bring up some of the issues on my list! A third problem with unstructured interviews is that it is very difficult to compare one person's answer with another's, for it might be that the reason that they didn't talk about a topic is not to do with them considering it unimportant, but because the interview didn't go that way.

So which …?

Well, as I've said more than once, there is no right way of interviewing and neither are the different types of interview necessarily exclusive. I suspect that many reading this book will tend to go for a semi-structured interview where you have a schedule of topics to discuss but where you can allow different interviews to develop in different ways. Certainly, if you are new to interviewing, then that would seem a wise way forward. As you build experience, so you may become more relaxed about how detailed to make your schedule of questions. Having said that, there are times when a structured approach to interviewing is more appropriate and when the benefits of that approach outweigh the benefits of flexibility in an unstructured interview. As you decide, keep in mind the objective that you've set for the interview: the purpose for which you want the information.

Conversations

I wonder if you have a mental image of an interview. Perhaps, the word conjures up a picture of an intense, confrontational television interview between a TV interviewer and a politician, or maybe you think of a chat-show host, or a short snippet of film such as a vox pop, as a TV reporter gets a comment from the 'ordinary people in the street'.

What these interviews all have in common is that they are formally organised; but a moment's thought will remind us of many informal conversations where we have learned something or heard new information. So in addition to formally organised interviews you will also find that informal conversations give you the scope for asking important questions.

For ease of discussion, I'll deal with these informal conversations under two headings, planned conversations and unplanned; but, to be honest, there isn't a hard dividing line between the two types.

Planned conversations

There are many reasons why you might choose not to conduct an interview with people, especially if you work with them. First, unless they're aware of your undertaking an educational project, the request for an 'interview' will seem just plain strange! And if it feels strange to them that may well affect what they say to you. Second, especially when you are undertaking a practice-centred inquiry, the people you might need to talk with may not believe they have the time for a formal interview, whereas they'll be relaxed 'chatting' with you for ten minutes. Thirdly, there may well be times when you don't want your informant to be aware that your questions to them are part of a coherent project. Now, this point raises some important issues about the ethics of an inquiry process and we'll have to return to that topic later in the book, but for now the point I want to make is that how open you are about your intentions in asking questions will affect the answers you are given, and this all has to go into the mix as you make sense of the information you gather through interviews.

So what are the important points to consider as you plan an informal conversation as a method for gathering information?

What's the best place and time?

I once had a manager who would always argue with me and try to show that any new idea of mine wasn't any good. He seemed determined to win arguments. So whenever I wanted to suggest a new idea to him, I'd find out when he would be on his way to a meeting and I'd 'chance' to bump into him in the corridor. 'Oh George,' I'd say, 'I know you haven't the time to talk now but I'm thinking of doing *xyz*.' (I'd mention some sort of new plan) 'could we talk about it later?' He'd say yes and hurry off to his meeting. Later he'd come to my office and always be in a different kind of mood. Somehow he'd want to

encourage me or, maybe, the idea had become his own. Whatever the reason, he would be far more open to the new idea and usually really helpful and wise. In the same way, if you are looking to ask a colleague, client or boss a question, you have to think what time and place would be the best to get a thoughtful and helpful answer. Maybe the canteen at lunchtime or just as work is slowing down at the end of a shift … you will have some ideas about the best time and place to ask your question.

How many questions can you ask?

This, again, is a question of judgement and you might have to change your mind at the very moment of a conversation! By and large you won't be able to ask too many questions without your respondent feeling 'got at', so think that through and be ready to read the signs if you're pressing your luck during the conversation. It might be worth trying to ask different questions on different occasions rather than trying to get every question asked at one time.

Declaring your intentions

This can be a tricky question and it leads back to the issue of our ethical responsibility, which I've discussed elsewhere. How much should you tell a colleague about your project before asking him or her your questions? There are several points to consider:

- Is it fair to use someone's thoughts in a project when they weren't aware of what you were doing?

- If they had known you were trying to do something they disagreed with, might they have given a different answer?

- Might you lose the sense of open and informal conversation if you indicate that there is a project lurking behind your 'innocent' question?

These are important questions of ethics and practicality. Seeking to balance the relative importance of each issue is not easy and will require some careful thinking.

Are you just a questioner or are you giving of yourself?

Just asking questions can create a very one-sided conversation. Sometimes, if you want someone to talk freely, then you will need to be open yourself. If you want someone to 'think out loud' then you may need to do the same or they will feel that you are taking advantage of them. This, however, causes a real quandary to an inquirer, for disclosing your own point of view on a matter might influence the answer you're given. There is no straightforward solution to this. If you were an external researcher coming into an organisation, it would be much easier to be detached and dispassionate, but practice-centred inquiries are generally done within your own organisation where the apparent objectivity that some researchers desire is just not possible. David Coghlan, in the reading 'Insider action research projects' at the end of this book, discusses this problem.

Unplanned conversations

Sometimes, almost out of the blue, a colleague or friend will say something that is really helpful to your inquiry and you will find yourself in a conversation that almost becomes an interview. On other occasions an opportunity will arise, perhaps because of a car journey together or over a cup of coffee, and you will be able to shape a conversation to help answer questions that are relevant to your inquiry. Now, you will need to be careful, of course, for if you get a reputation for steering every chance conversation towards your 'pet project', very soon *nobody* will be willing to chat with you! However, do be attentive to opportunities that present themselves. One thing that I've found helpful is to carry a small notebook around with me where I can jot down interesting comments that I'd like to recall. We'll see that that notebook is also helpful if we're doing observational research.

Interviewing skills

Interviewing, whether in formal settings or within informal conversations, is a skilled activity. It's something that we get better at with practice. So don't worry if you don't feel very skilled at asking questions to begin with; you **will** get better, but getting better requires you to do two things: first, get started even if you don't do it perfectly; and second, once you've begun, notice and attend to the areas where you need to improve. Here are some common areas where you will need to think and work carefully to become a skilled interviewer.

Asking clear questions

I've mentioned this a couple of times already but it bears repeating; you do have to work at making sure that your questions are clear to your respondent. Sometimes what is obvious to you is less clear to others. So try out your questions on friends first; do they see what you're getting at? Also, be careful about asking questions that are too simple; sometimes your respondent might think that you are trying to 'get at something' hidden. But remember that short questions are nearly always better than long, rambling questions that you need to explain.

Listening

This may seem obvious but it is so easy to hear what you want to hear rather than what is actually being said. Additionally, in less structured interviews, you need to listen carefully for signs that your respondent might want to say more or that they might want to shift the question a little. Is this a diversion or a valid shift in perspective? There are other times when your respondent will need some encouragement to tell their story – they might not be sure if you want to hear it! Listening inevitably involves us in making judgements about what we want or

this: you will always have to consider the implications of asking questions for your on-going relations.

The opportunity to ask questions will often pop up most unexpectedly

Of course, often you will plan a more formal conversation, but as I mentioned in the section 'Unplanned conversations', sometimes you will just find yourself with the chance to gather some really helpful information. There's no way of planning such occasions, and you will have to develop 'antennae' to spot them. This skill, as with so much of interviewing, comes with practice, but do help yourself by looking for opportunities.

So how can you manage these issues?

I'm afraid that there is little advice that I can give on this question, for the answer will depend very much on your particular work context and the nature of your on-going relations with colleagues, friends and social contacts. In the end, your management of a work-based, productive inquiry will be down to your own judgement of what to do. Perhaps the following questions will help you make those judgements:

- Is getting a partial answer better than taking risks in order to get a 'perfect' answer?

- Would you like another person to treat you as you propose to treat a colleague when asking them questions?

- How do you balance a need to make progress with your project with a desire for better information?

Summary

In this chapter we have explored the various ways of gathering information by asking people questions. I have categorised this in different ways: formal interviews and informal conversations; structured, semi-structured and unstructured interviews and, finally, planned and unplanned conversations. In each case we've thought about the benefits and problems of using each of these methods and I've sought to give clues for how to decide between the different types of interview and the skills needed to do each of them successfully.

... and finally

I am conscious that this has been a long and detailed chapter with many issues to be balanced and considered. I wonder if the whole process seems intimidating. There are two points to make here, which I hope will encourage you. First, even if you make a mistake, the nature of a productive inquiry will generally give you an opportunity to recover. The repeated cycles of inquiry will always give you an opportunity for testing and improving the information you have gathered and your understanding of that material. Second, I have stressed that productive inquiry is a gradual process and there are techniques that will help you constantly improve the quality of your understanding and information gathering. In particular, the process of **theoretical sampling**, which I introduce in Chapter 8, will help you in this process. A crucial point about asking questions is that it's a skilled process, like playing the piano, playing tennis or working with computers. You get better at it! But only if you get started and learn from experience!

7 Methods of inquiry: other sources of information

Introduction

Although asking people questions will undoubtedly form a major part of any productive inquiry, there are other sources of information that we can use to build up our sense of what is going on and how we should act in any particular circumstance. Remember that what we are trying to do in an inquiry that centres on our work practice is to enrich the way we are making sense of our and other people's actions, so that we can improve our effectiveness within a particular work context. So we need to be alert to information from a number of sources.

In this chapter we'll look in some detail at three methods that have become associated with ethnographic research:

- Using published materials, for example:
  - organisational documents: emails, memos, reports etc.
  - public databases
  - newspapers, journals, annual reports
- Noticing artefacts: the things around us that can give an impression about our work context
- Observing others' actions and talk.

Using published materials

Statistical databases and reports

Remember, we will focus mostly on what is called qualitative inquiry methods, so we will not be exploring ways of designing questionnaires or surveys. However, that does not mean that we can't find, gather or use numerical data in our inquiry. Statistics can help answer different kinds of questions. Consider the following three examples:

- Your inquiry involves you trying out a new sales technique; say, visiting customers more frequently or attempting to get into a new market. In this case, it would make sense to look at your sales figures, over a period of a few weeks or months.
- You're interested in working with young people in your town; in this case it would make sense to look at government census figures to

see how many young people live in your area and whether they're predominantly in, say, the under 13s or over 15s. You might also be able to find projected trends for demographic changes.

- You're trying to improve staff retention at your company. You make some changes to your recruitment strategy. So, over the next few months, you keep a record of starters, leavers and the average length of employment. What are the trends following the changes you've made? Are people staying longer or are they still going after three months?

Activity 7.1

15 minutes

First, think about your own job or involvement in a social organisation. Could you make a list of questions that you could ask about your work that would have numerical answers? Second, think about what statistics are widely available, both within your organisation and in the public domain?

Comment

In answering the first question, you need to remember the issue of cost, particularly in terms of time. A couple of the questions could easily be answered by a research survey but that might not be practicable. So the second question becomes more important: what statistics are easily available? For students studying at the Open University, the library and information services have a significant array of government and other published statistics. There is also an online tutorial that helps you learn how to access this material.

Some issues to consider in using published material

Published material, in the form of statistical reports and databases can be immensely helpful to anyone involved in a productive inquiry. They can give access to detailed information that would cost a great deal in both cash and time, so, if at all possible, do make use of it. However, you will need to take care, for there are some important issues to be considered in how you understand these figures:

- Statistics are always gathered for a purpose and that purpose might not be the same as your own. So, for example, some market research might have been done for a particular company and its

range of products, which might refer to a market somewhat different from your own. To take an example uncomfortably close to home for me: recently a group representing university authorities published figures showing that some universities are facing serious financial problems. Could it possibly be that the publication of these reports has anything to do with the next round of pay negotiations starting shortly? In understanding publicly produced reports, you will need to consider if their purpose might affect their relevance to your own inquiry.

- Most importantly, the definitions used by a public body or market research firm might differ from your own. Some examples of this might include:
  - different definitions of market, industrial or geographic sector
  - different time periods
  - different financial definitions.

I remember a little while ago I was doing some work for an engineering firm who worked in the metal pressings industry (working with firms who produced products like spoons, brackets or fasteners – any product where metal is bent into a specific shape). When I started to look for some market research information, I found that metal pressings were grouped with forgings, which included a very different array of companies. I had to be careful in how I understood the material I read as much of it was irrelevant to my own inquiry.

- Further questions arise over the source of a report. It is worth asking if the author of a report is likely or able to tell the full truth. To help understand this, take a look at Activity 7.2.

- A key question in considering the above points is whether you can find any corroboration of these figures. Are there any statistics produced by another group? Or can you speak with people who could confirm or challenge the figures and the possible interpretations that might be given to them?

Activity 7.2

15 minutes

Consider the following examples of published documents and assess how likely the authors of each were to publish the full, balanced and truthful account:

a company annual report

a product brochure

a political party's election manifesto

a trade union's report on pay comparisons

a university academic's official research report.

Comment

I would want to stress that I'm not saying that any of these publications are deceitful in any way. No one is necessarily lying but it is likely that figures will be reported in such a way as to put a particular 'gloss' on them, given the publishing body's own agenda. Of course, I would like to say that the one exception to all this is the academic researcher, but we have our own perspectives, careers and needs for funding just like anyone else. So, even in this case, you will need to be careful how you interpret what you read.

Reading documents in practice-centred inquiry

For many of us, working life is filled with paperwork, even if it comes to us electronically. Indeed, email has increased the amount of information that we're handling considerably. For the practice-centred inquirer, this can provide a rich source of information for building up your sense of what is going on and what actions are desirable and feasible. So what sort of documents might you consider using?

- Email correspondence
  - Don't forget to ask colleagues for their emails, if that would be acceptable.
- Memos – where they still exist!

- Minutes and agendas of meetings
  - Now, these can be very interesting, especially if you are able to compare the formal minutes with your own notes of a meeting. There are occasions when the formal minutes provide what might be considered the official gloss on a meeting. If that is the case, then it might well be informative to consider contrasts with less formal recollections of the minutes. Such considerations might give powerful insights into what actions are going to gain managerial support and which won't. We'll discuss this later in the chapter, when we cover the use of multiple inquiry methods.
  - Minutes can also be interesting in terms of what actions they suggest others will be taking over a period of time.
  - Agendas can also give an indication of colleagues' priorities. Of course, some agendas contain just the regular headings and so aren't particularly interesting, but checking up for the occasions when the regular pattern is changed can be insightful.
- Reports
  - Some organisations are keen on reports and others aren't. If you work for one of those where reports are written about all and any topic, these might well provide you with useful information.
  - A close relation to reports are presentations. We'll discuss these in more detail when we cover 'observation' methods, but for now, I just want to issue a warning about using

PowerPoint presentations and bullet points in particular (ahem, Caroline, what are these in your book here!). The problem is that bullet point lists often give you the headings without the background thinking. Consequently, you may very well find that you are 'reading meanings into' what are very short bits of text.

- o Of course, if your inquiry is centred on some area of your work where monthly sales, financial or production reports could be helpful, then don't forget to use these.

Activity 7.3 asks you to think about the kind of reports your own organisation produces.

- Orders, invoices and other commercial documentation
  - o In some cases your inquiry project might benefit from this kind of information. There are often details on orders and invoices that can be significant.

Activity 7.3

5 minutes

Jot down a list of the kind of regular reports that your organisation produces that might be helpful to a practice-based inquiry you might undertake.

Comment

I'm on the committee of my sailing club which uses a big reservoir in the Midlands of England. We have a series of monthly reports to consider: financial figures, accident reports, details of new members and lists of those who have lapsed their membership. We also produce some irregular reports; for example, on the costs of running big races for visiting sailors or on the costs of redesigning the reservoir shore to help more boats get on the water quickly. We also have occasional reports from the water company from whom we lease the water.

Noticing artefacts

What counts as an artefact when you're thinking about a practice-centred inquiry? Well, yet again, I'd have to say that there is no one correct answer to this question. Have you noticed how often I've found myself writing that? Essentially, when talking about artefacts, I'm thinking of those items that can be of symbolic importance and might give some indication of what is considered important in a working context; what is valued, or something about the style of an organisation or person. So, for example, if I'm interviewing a person who I've never met before, I tend to look around their office to pick up hints as to their background.

Activity 7.4

15 minutes

You enter the office of two executives in a local government agency. Here are descriptions of their working space.

Working space 1

This is a small but pleasant single-occupancy office. On one wall, within reach of the desk chair, is a well-stocked bookshelf with a collection of professional books, magazines and box files of papers. The desk itself is a little untidy but not excessively so, and on the pinboard are photos of children and a couple of examples of children's crayon drawings. The desk has a small bowl of freesias, near to the end of their life.

Working space 2

This is a desk in an open-plan office. The desk itself is extremely tidy with files of papers apparently colour coded and carefully clipped together. Whilst the desk is identical to others in the office, the desk chair is different, having a high-back, executive look to it. There are sound panels around the working space and on one of them is an array of work documents that appear, without careful reading, to be statements of company policy. There are no pictures around, although on the desk is some sort of trophy with either a squash or badminton racquet on it.

So what do you think you can say about the people who work at these two stations?

Comment

Well, it would be very easy to work with stereotypes here, wouldn't it? And this is an important point when working with artefacts, for your interpretation of them is likely to say as much about you as about the people who put the artefacts in place. Consequently, when using artefacts in inquiry and seeking to interpret their meaning and significance, you will almost certainly need to have other information. You will not be able to work with these artefacts alone.

So, for example, it might be possible to intuit from the descriptions above that the first person is a caring, family person, perhaps somewhat academic in their manner, whilst the second is a harder, competitive rule-keeper who is more senior within the context of an open-plan working space. Two points to consider here: first, how does my description tie in with yours? What other interpretations are possible (for example, is the high-backed chair not a sign of seniority but the provision by occupational health for someone with a bad back)? Second, as you get into the interview the words of your respondent might either re-affirm your initial insights or contradict them. However, if used with care, the insights offered by artefacts can be helpful.

Here are some examples of artefacts; you may very well want to note down other examples that would be relevant in your own working context.

Working conditions

If you're trying to understand the way an organisation works, for example, it might be significant whether or not levels of hierarchy are signified by office furniture, workspace, the size of desk and so on. At one company where I worked, directors had two window offices, managers had one window with two pillars, assistant managers had a window with only one pillar and the rest of us were crammed into multi-user offices. At another firm I worked at, it was proudly stated that everyone had exactly the same office furniture. Was there any difference between these companies and their views of hierarchy and authority? Well, to make that judgement you'd have to ask some questions, but your initial sensemaking might help you word those questions so that you can test your initial assumptions.

Organisational symbols

Many organisations have created symbols or brands that are supposed to tell a story about the organisation. One company I worked for sponsored a Formula One racing team. The story that the firm wanted to project was that they were leaders in their own technology field, just like the racing team. Now, there is a problem with using symbols to tell you anything: it might be that the symbol is saying what certain senior managers *wished* that the organisation were like! It may be very far removed from the particular aspect of the department where you work or from whom you are seeking to get information.

I remember that at another place where I worked, the company logo was used as a coat hook and at Christmas a bauble was hung from it. Were these signs of disrespect for the company, perhaps a little mark of rebellion? My memory of our chat within that office suggests to me that it showed a little cynicism together with some light-hearted fun!

Now, the point to make here is that both of these stories tell us something about the organisations involved. However, to be honest, I'm not sure what they say! Notice how, in the second story, I added to the symbol; how it was mocked and also some memories of the kinds of conversations that we had there. In a way, although I wasn't engaged in any kind of research then, I was using a method called **triangulation**, in that I used different methods of gathering inquiry material to confirm or test sense that I was beginning to make of a situation.

Workspace

How is workspace laid out? Who works near whom? Is a factory located near its suppliers or customers? Is access to senior managers through a secretary's office? Is it easy to 'pop by' a colleague or do they work in another building? Each of these questions, and I'm sure you could think of many more, can help you build a picture or story of what's going on. For example, might poor communications between departments be linked to them being located in different parts of a large, office campus?

Types of wall furnishings

Are there works of art, pictures of founding 'fathers' of the firm? Perhaps there are posters that exhort workers to greater efforts, graphs showing production levels or lists of company or health and safety regulations. There again, there may be personal posters or advertisements for 'works' social clubs. What is on the walls might well tell you something about the people who work in that place.

Activity 7.5

15 minutes

I once worked for a company that had a huge picture of a lion across the entrance to its factory. Underneath was printed: 'In our business the customer is king'. At a university I worked at a few years ago, the corridor walls were covered in glass cabinets with endless student lists and course instructions with deadline dates.

Imagine that you are working at those two sites and conducting an inquiry into how to improve communications. Having noticed the details that I've mentioned, what sort of inquiries would you make in the organisations?

Comment

Now, I would stress that my ideas are not the only ways of undertaking the inquiry, but I suspect that I would be interested in the following.

(a) At the 'customer is king' factory, what do the workforce think of the poster? Perhaps more importantly, I'd wonder if such a poster makes the factory employees feel valued. I might wonder at such an all-embracing poster, and wonder if this is the only way that the management communicates with staff. Do the workers feel that they are talked to on an individual basis or do they just feel part of 'the workforce'? I think that my interest would be to check if this poster makes people feel talked with or talked at, whether it makes them feel anonymous or a valued individual, and so whether they feel personally responsible for the quality of their work or just a cog in a machine. You see, from other reading that I've done, I just wonder if such a poster might even have a contradictory result and actually contribute to people not caring so much about the quality of their work!

(b) At the university, I think that I'd want to see how many of the students actually stop to read these notices. I'd want to find out if these notices were a genuinely thought-out way of communicating with students or a fall-back position, enabling tutors to say, 'Well, you should have known about the assignment – I put details of it on the notice-board.' I'd also want to find out about other forms of communication; for example, do students come to lectures or seminars? What about email and other electronic forms of communication: do tutors and/or students use them?

These examples are not exhaustive; I'm sure that you could add to them. Notice how the artefacts did not tell me any certain facts, but they did provoke a series of questions for me to follow in my inquiry. So, artefacts are not foolproof methods of finding out what's going on in any particular work context. Rather, they are clues or hints. They can play two important roles in an inquiry:

1 They can help you **identify possible lines of inquiry**; they might provoke you into questioning aspects of your work context that you had previously not noticed. They also might cause you to question some of your current sensemaking about your work context and your own practice within that context.

2 They can also **illustrate conclusions** that you had reached by using different inquiry methods. In one way, they can add some richness to your description of what's going on; in another, they might help you illustrate, and so empower, your efforts to persuade others of your action.

What is very important about this, however, is that you incorporate the use of artefacts within an on-going process of testing your emerging sense of what is going on. I will discuss this in greater depth in the next chapter.

Definition: Triangulation

Triangulation in research methods is the technique of using different methods whilst inquiring into a situation of issue. In a way, it is like looking at a place from a different perspective. You get to see the same place, situation or event from a different point of view. So, for example, an inquirer might observe a meeting and then interview participants of that meeting to seek their view of it. Another example might be that having interviewed members of a manufacturing unit, who told you that production was increasing week by week, you then go and dig out the monthly production records to see if those figures confirm what you've heard in interviews.

Essentially, there are two ways of using the triangulation of methods. First, you can use it to test the **accuracy** of an emerging sense of what is going on. In this case, you would use a second inquiry method to test your current understanding of what is happening by looking for evidence in a different way. Alternatively, you might well use more than one inquiry method to give you a more **detailed** view. Perhaps, here, a good analogy would be how we use our eyes. We can see what's going on around us through one eye, but using two eyes enables us to see things in more depth; using two eyes allows us to gauge distances better. We get

> to see the world in 3-D, so to speak. Triangulation – the use of multiple methods – can have the same benefit for us.

Observing action and conversation

The role of the observer

A central element of classical ethnography was the conducting of observational research, to record and give an account of what was going on in any particular situation or period of time. At the time of its origins, ethnographic research was done by western anthropologists trying to learn about non-western communities and cultures. Consequently, the process of observation was always being carried out by an outsider, someone who wasn't a part of the local community. However, as soon as ethnographic methods started to be used within western contexts or by non-western researchers looking at their own cultures, some of the assumptions about how best to carry out observational research started to be challenged.

In the initial anthropological studies, the researcher was very much an outsider to the community they were studying and we could say that they were **non-participant observers**. However, in organisational studies, much of the work – for example, Tony Watson's (1994) study of managers at a large telephone manufacturing site – has been done by people who are actively involved in the organisation and who we can call **participant observers**. For those involved in a productive inquiry, any observation will almost certainly be done within a participant frame, but it may be that on occasion you'll 'sit in' on a meeting as a non-participant. The crucial practical difference between the two frames is how you understand your own influence upon what you see. To take a silly example: if you hand out biscuits to all the participants at a meeting, it really wouldn't be a profound insight to write, 'All participants in the meeting ate biscuits'! Of course, in reality, an inquirer's influence on people's actions will tend to be much more subtle and sometimes hidden. In the next chapter, I will introduce the research process of reflexivity which is a vital part of how we can make sense of the information we gather by observational methods.

Techniques for improving the quality of your observation

So how can you carry out the most useful observational inquiry? How can you make sure that you remember as much of what you see as possible? It's amazing how quickly we forget the important details of an event or situation – the overall impression stays but the details seem to go almost as soon as we see them.

Activity 7.6

15 minutes

Think back over the last few days and select a meeting, conversation, event or situation. Start by writing a one-sentence summary of what happened or perhaps why it was important. Next, try to write down exactly what happened.

Comment

I suspect that you found it easy enough to recall your overall impression of what happened, but as you tried to write down the detail several problems probably occurred. You might recognise some of them in my example below.

To explain, I'll use an example of a meeting that I ran yesterday. It was a training meeting that had some good moments but also some moments when things seemed to go awry.

Now, I was a participant observer (I was the consultant running the training), so I had to be very sensitive to what was going on in the conversation. As a result I found it difficult to note down **exactly what was said**. Later, as I wrote up my notes I found that there were moments when particular participants said something important but I couldn't remember their exact words.

Early on in the meeting, I had thought that it was very significant that the participants weren't answering a particular question of mine. In a later conversation, one participant had mentioned that he had totally misunderstood what I was on about. The significance of that earlier moment was now very different. So, in writing up my notes, I had to decide on a **narrative style** that noted my initial surprise at my question not being answered, and also my later embarrassment as I realised that this may have been because I had got the question wrong! In the end, I put the two events together in one paragraph rather than writing them down separately according to their **chronological order**. I do wonder, however, if in doing that I downplayed my earlier understanding of what had been happening.

From earlier meetings in this project, I'd noticed how we tended to move away from the focus of individual management skills and towards one that looked to solve particular organisational problems. On several occasions incidents like this came up. Now, in my notes taken during the meeting, I focused on the conversations with each individual concerned. I had set out my notes with their names as headings and noted down what was said under those different sections. Later, as I tidied up these rough notes into a more coherent record, I found again that I was struggling to remember the chronological order, and I had to work quite hard to recall if particular things had been said before or after another significant conversation, when I had pointed out what we were doing and sought to change the direction of our conversation.

Now, let's take some of the events and problems I mentioned above and see what advice might help in the keeping of field notes.

Field notes

The keeping of field notes is absolutely vital to doing a good productive inquiry. You'll have noticed that I commented a couple of times about *rough notes* and then how I *wrote them up* more tidily. I tend to keep a small notebook in my handbag so that I can surreptitiously note down important events or comments. At the meeting I've described, however, I had a larger, A4 notebook, which gave me more opportunity to jot down diagrams and make my notes more open. Still, rough notes will not be good enough when you want to work on your inquiry a few weeks later, so you will need to write them up into a tidier form as soon after the meeting (event, conversation, whatever …) as possible. I tend to do this on my computer because word processor packages have some useful tools (like word searches or cut and paste) that may be useful as I rearrange the details and try to make sense of my notes. Sometimes this is not possible; for example, yesterday I wasn't able to get to my computer for the rest of the day and I'm not sure that I'll be able to find the time to work on this project again for a few days now. So I sat down in a café and re-wrote my notes longhand. I'll re-do these on my computer in a day or so.

Structuring your notes

There are various ways that you can structure your notes and your observation. Three very common ones are:

- chronological order
- particular actions
- particular people.

I could have ordered my rough notes before the meeting by splitting them up into, say, one-, two-, or five-minute chunks. I would then have written down what happened in each time chunk. Doing this would have helped me make sure that I knew when the particular conversations happened. However, given that I was running the meeting, it would have been virtually impossible for me to keep such a detailed record. As is so often the case in an inquiry, there are trade-offs to be made and you will have to make judgements about what is more important to you in any given situation.

So what I did was to structure my notes around the individuals I was working with. This meant that I had pretty good notes about the issues I discussed with each participant. However, I still struggled to get really detailed notes of the actual words used in comments. If I hadn't been an active participant in the meeting, I would have been more able to take down exact notes.

A third method that I could have used for structuring my notes would have been to focus on a particular activity. So, for example, since the questions I ask are an important part of the project, I could have focused on those, noting down how people responded to each of my questions.

Sometimes it is possible to identify before an observation exactly what it is that you're looking for. For example, maybe you are researching manager relations with staff and to do that you attend a meeting where a manager is giving feedback to her team. In that case, you might create different categories of actions, such as smiling, listening, encouraging and censuring. You could then note down the number of times the manager did each of the category actions. Of course, the problem with this method is that you might be focusing so much on your preset action-categories that you don't notice other important activities in the meeting.

Involving others in the observation

One of the problems that I noted in my account of yesterday's meeting was that I was so busy leading the meeting that I didn't have time to note down the details of what was happening during the meeting. One way that I could have handled this problem would have been to ask another person to act as an observer; to do that I would have had to have helped them know what to look for. I chose not to do this for two reasons. First, all the other meeting participants were there to be trained and I didn't think that it would have been fair to distract them from their learning. Second, if I had asked for a non-participant observer to help me, there would also have been problems since some of the issues that we discussed were confidential. As you consider the best way of managing an observational inquiry, you will also have options such as these, but there are trade-offs to be considered. It will be very rare for one option to be entirely without problems.

Another way that I could have involved others to help with my observations would have been to ask another participant to observe what was going on and then to get together to compare notes of what we thought had been going on. In an informal way, I did actually do this during a conversation with one of the participants after the meeting. I checked some points with him to see how he responded to my thoughts about the meeting. This conversation turned out to be very helpful, as it was during this conversation that he pointed out that he had misunderstood the question that I referred to in my account. If you are observing a meeting yourself, look around and see if there are others who could help you or if there is someone you could ask for comments later.

One other way of getting other people's help is to ask them to keep diaries or journals of their activities. Of course, it has to be said that

you might need to be very persuasive to get them to do this, but there might be occasions when some people would be willing. As with other methods, the information that you get from these diaries or journals would have to be interpreted, for apart from anything else, your respondent might use the diary as a way of making a particular point. Whilst I confess to being sceptical about the diary-keeping method, there may be circumstances when it could provide you with some really good information.

Rich descriptions

What do you include in your notes of an observation? Well, in an ideal world the answer to that question is everything; but that is unlikely to be possible. If you are able to be a non-participant observer, then try to include as much as you can. If in doubt, noting it down would be good advice. You can always drop material that on further consideration is unimportant.

Here are some hints as to what you could include:

The physical context

> Note the layout of the room, where people are sitting (who's sitting next to whom?), the comfort or otherwise of the room and the facilities (is there coffee, tea, water?).

The people involved

> Who are they? Does their body language suggest that they are fully engaged or distant? Is anyone significant *not* there?

The conversations

> Who talks, who's silent? Is the conversation good-natured or angry? What is actually said? Do certain people get involved in only *some* conversational topics? Or are there particular people involved in every conversation?

Particular events

> People entering/leaving the room, sudden (or gradual) changes in tempo and phone calls.

Yourself

> Do include yourself in your observation: how were you feeling? What interested you or bored you? How did you impact on the meeting/situation?

I suspect that I could go on for many, many pages and I'd still leave some important factors out, so the above list is only there to get you thinking.

Multi-methods

Over the last couple of chapters we have looked at several different inquiry methods for gathering information. An important point to make in finishing this short overview of inquiry methods is that they are not exclusive. Just because you intend to ask people questions in formal interviews does not mean that you can't have informal conversations with colleagues after you have observed them interact in a meeting or whilst doing their work. Indeed, academic researchers would go further and positively encourage you to use multiple methods. This is for two reasons:

- *Access*

There are times when it just might not be possible to get access to a meeting that you would be keen to observe. In that case, you may have to make do with some conversations with participants to find out what went on. Or it might be that you are keen to see some market research data, but all you can actually get your hands on is an internal summary report of the data.

Productive inquiry is governed by what is possible and this is especially the case when time is short. You may have to improvise, make do and mend, be creative in making use of what comes to hand. The best advice is to keep your eyes open for every opportunity to enrich your collection of information.

- *Triangulation*

An additional reason for using multiple inquiry methods is the technique that I referred to earlier called triangulation. This is a process by which you can test out some information that you've been given. Say, for example, that a colleague told you that the marketing manager was unhappy with the current brochure. You might well want to test out this information, and several different methods might be useful for doing so. You could ask the marketing manager herself, or you could take the brochure to other colleagues and see what they thought. It might be that the marketing manager is a lone voice. Still another method, if it were possible, would be to take the brochure to a group of prospective customers (called a focus group) and see what they thought of it.

Each of these different methods would add different perspectives, and confirm or challenge your emerging sense of what is going on. Triangulation as an inquiry method takes us into the area of our making sense of the information that we have gathered. In the next chapter we will come across a process called **theoretical sampling,** where we do something similar to triangulation as we test our emerging understanding of what is going on and seek either to confirm the ideas and actions that we are taking or challenge those ideas and actions. Together, theoretical sampling (deciding where best to go next for information) and triangulation (using different ways of looking at the same events, situations or ideas) will help you in the difficult process of making sound judgements about the actions you need to take in a productive inquiry. It is to that process of making sense of information to which we turn next.

Summary

In this chapter we have covered the following methods of inquiry:

- Using published materials, for example:
  - organisational documents such as emails, memos and reports
  - public databases
  - newspapers, journals, annual reports
- Noticing artefacts: the things around us that can give us an impression about our work context
- Observing others' actions and talk.

A crucial theme that has come through when discussing each of these methods is that they do not provide us with failsafe information. Making sense of the information we gather, the topic of the next chapter, will be difficult and involves making judgements about how to interpret what we see, hear and read. We will have to judge how much weight to give to different types of information. In this chapter, I suggested that one way of helping us deal with this difficulty is to use multiple methods and seek to 'triangulate' information from different methods. I also pointed out the crucial importance of keeping good field notes (sigh, remember that advice yourself, Caroline!), for good field notes will help you revisit your information time and time again, comparing it with other information and enriching your sensemaking process.

8 Making sense of your information

Aims of this chapter

In this chapter we focus our attention on methods that will help us make sense of the information that we have gathered using a range of inquiry methods. I'll suggest a sequence of activities to help you through the process of making sense of information, which is then followed by a choice between taking action and seeking further information.

Introduction

So, you've interviewed people; perhaps you've done some observation and collected some artefacts and statistical reports. How do you make sense of all this material?

I'd like to make two points to begin with. First, you're too late; you should have been making sense of the material throughout the inquiry! (But then, I hope you're reading this book before you've got too far with your inquiry, so you should be all right!) I wouldn't be surprised if you find it helpful to read the previous two chapters again after reading this chapter. I would remind you again of the basic tool that I've set up for undertaking a productive inquiry: the cycle of inquiry, where you take action and then reflect on what happened as you took action and the consequences of that action. The reflection process is one of making sense of the information that you are gathering.

Second, the process of interpreting, analysing or, as I will call it for the rest of the book, 'sensemaking' is the topic of this chapter. As in our earlier discussions about inquiry, there are as many different opinions held about analysing, interpreting or making sense of research material as there are researchers. The very fact that I've used three terms alerts us to quite different perspectives about the research or inquiry process.

Analysing   suggests a detached and objective process where a rational analyst uses 'scientific' methods to untangle a web of different bits of data to come up with a correct, dispassionate, objective analysis and description of what is going on in a particular situation. The major argument in favour of an analytical approach is that it may help you avoid 'seeing what you want to see'. Especially in a productive inquiry, when you will probably have invested much of yourself in the project, it will help you to consciously try to detach yourself from your information, and seek to be as objective as you can be.

Interpreting   carries with it an impression that the researcher might not be so detached and objective about their 'data'. To simplify a complicated debate, there are two reasons why a researcher might expect to interpret material rather than analyse it.

First, data might be conflicting and confusing. There might be a need to distinguish between relevant and irrelevant, significant or insignificant data. These decisions are a process of interpretation and will, to a large extent, depend on the starting assumptions or perspective of a researcher.

Second, a researcher might take a somewhat different view of the relationship between research material and the researcher, arguing that we are never able to see everything that's going on. At the very best, we will only ever be able to see from one perspective and so, even when we do something that looks and feels analytical, it will still involve an element of interpretation.

Now, I need to declare an interest here. I am not writing this book as an unbiased observer of this debate. I am, as a researcher myself, very much in the thick of the discussion and I find myself strongly within that latter interpretative perspective. So you'll have to read what I write in this chapter bearing in mind the perspective from which I write.

Apart from my own intellectual roots, there is another reason for a practice-centred inquiry to be a process of sensemaking and interpretion. As you inquire into your practice, you will find that you will never have all the information you need before you have to take your next action. You will not be able to carry on gathering information until you hit the point, called 'saturation' by some researchers, where you have enough information to come to a final conclusion about what is going on and why it is happening that way. You will be involved in a productive inquiry, trying to make things happen and conducting your inquiry around your actions. Sometimes there will hardly be a chance to reflect before taking action! Consequently, the sense you are able to make of what is going on around you and your contribution to that activity will always be partial or emergent.

Now, within the field of qualitative research, two traditions of research offer methods that help to deal with this emergent process of understanding. These two traditions are called grounded theory and ethnography. Both these research methodologies have much to offer a productive inquiry and you will notice a similarity with the key process of action research: the action-reflection cycle of inquiry.

As I write this chapter, I will refer frequently to a large research project that I was involved in recently. I spent about two years working in a university team seeking ways to help a large engineering firm called Premier Engineering to develop some of their management processes, so that they could take advantage of new computer systems.

The centrality of testing your emerging sensemaking

In their somewhat different ways, both grounded theory and ethnography shape inquiry around an emergent process of making sense of the situation, activity or issue into which the researcher is inquiring. Both methodologies emphasise this emergent nature of sensemaking. There are three reasons why I would like to emphasise this emergence.

First,   we cannot expect to fully appreciate or understand what is going on at our first inquiry. We will come to an initial, partial judgement or theory of what is 'going on around here', but the information upon which we base this judgement will be incomplete and we will need to test, refine and enrich our sensemaking.

Second,   as Strauss came to appreciate, we never come to any inquiry as a *tabula rasa*; that is, with a totally clear and objective starting point. Especially when undertaking a practice-centred inquiry, we are most likely to have been working in an organisation for a while beforehand. Consequently, we will start with opinions and judgements that will be a convoluted mix of fact, bias, assumption and informed judgement. As we start our inquiry into our own practice, it will be wise to test out just how robust our current sensemaking is.

Third,   a practice-centred inquiry does not take place within a fixed context. As we continue our inquiry, taking new actions, those actions will affect the work context. People may change both positively or negatively in response to our actions. The situation in general may change as quite possibly unrelated actions impinge upon our practice and work context. It pays, therefore, to keep testing our sense of what is going in to ensure that it is keeping pace with changing circumstances.

The stages of sensemaking

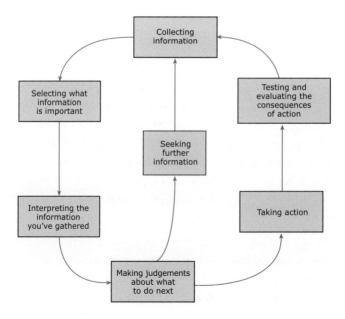

Figure 8.1 The process of sensemaking

Figure 8.1 provides a model of the process by which we can make sense during a productive inquiry. Let's outline each stage briefly, and then we'll spend a bit longer on some of the methods that researchers have developed over the years that may help you go through these different stages.

Collecting information

Hopefully, we don't need to spend time discussing this activity, since we covered it pretty fully in the previous two chapters. Within the context of sensemaking, I would only want to re-emphasise the point that some information will come to us in three ways.

First,   we'll come across information in the course of our daily, working lives. We might not be looking for it especially, but some occurrence or something said by a colleague will strike us as relevant to our inquiry, so we'll note it down to think about later. The skill to learn here is to be sensitive to what is going on around you and events or comments that might have a bearing on your research. Marshall (1999; 2001) writes of **inner and outer arcs of attention**. (I have included one of Marshall's papers, 'Living life as inquiry', in the Readings section at the end of this book.)

What I find particularly valuable about Marshall's thinking is that phrase 'arc of attention'. This is what is so often required in research; just paying attention to what is going on around us. It sounds so simple, but in practice it isn't that easy. For most of us, there is a need to practise noticing. We notice inner arcs of attention when we focus on our own feelings, responses or thoughts within a particular situation. Whilst such thoughts, feelings and responses are very subjective, and so will need to be tested as to their value, they can be very helpful within an inquiry. Outer arcs of attention include noting what others around us are doing and saying.

Second,   we'll actively go looking for information about a particular question that we're asking. This is a process of helping us think about what to do. We'll have more to say about this below when we discuss **theoretical sampling**.

Third,   when we've taken action, we'll need to find information that will help us evaluate the consequences of that action.

Now, the point I want to make here is that the *reason* for your collecting information will tend to shape what you notice. You might say that actually collecting information is a part of the interpretative process we're undertaking. This is one of the reasons that I've suggested you might want to re-read the inquiry methods chapters again after reading this chapter. This aspect of our understanding of information that we have gathered draws our attention to one of the key features of any inquiry. The way that we think, our values and the questions we ask will all shape what we see, hear and notice. They will also affect how we go about interpreting the information that we've gathered.

'It's a puzzle to me.'

This is a problem for an inquirer, for how can we know that the information that we've gathered is true and not just a projection of our own assumptions and prejudices? Essentially, answers to this question have boiled down to two categories. First, there are those researchers who place emphasis on the correct use of research methods. For this group, the aspiration is that skilled use of research methods will enable an inquirer to establish an objective position with regards to the issues that they are examining. A second group of researchers argue that this objectivity is not possible and suggest, instead, that any inquirer must engage a **reflexive** approach to their research.

Definition: Reflexivity

In discussing the activities of asking questions and observation, and our interpretation of the meaning and importance of artefacts, I have emphasised how we can shape both what we 'see' and how we understand what we see. Whilst some academic researchers still seek to be as objective as they can be in using these different methods, it is generally accepted amongst qualitative researchers that this isn't possible. Consequently, qualitative researchers have developed the process of reflexivity, by which they openly discuss and reflect upon the impact that they are having on their emerging sense of what is going on. For people involved in productive inquiry, the need for reflexivity is very important as well, but for a slightly different reason from that of the academic researcher. For a productive inquiry, there is a need to check that our own subjective sensemaking is not too far removed from the sensemaking of others with whom we are working.

There are three ways in which you can use reflexivity within a productive inquiry.

1   In being explicit about how you might have influenced what you 'saw' or 'heard', you can give yourself the chance to weigh up the quality of the information that you have noted down. This, in turn, can then inform how you continue with your inquiry, perhaps suggesting ways of testing your initial understanding of information.

2   Various methods that I'll discuss during this chapter become ways through which you can test, reflexively, your gathering and interpretation of information. In particular, the method of looking for **negative cases** can help, as can the process of **theoretical sampling**. Of course, finally, the action research **cycles of inquiry** will give an indication of the quality of your information as your actions either work or don't work. What is necessary, however, for all of these methods to be helpful is that *first recognition* that there might be a problem with the accuracy of the information you have gathered and that you adopt a reflexive attitude to your own inquiry. We will discuss all these methods later in this chapter.

3   A final tool that will be helpful in keeping your inquiry reflexive is a reflective team or individual; someone to whom you can

---

> take your inquiry, evidence and emerging sensemaking and get a different perspective. You have several options here. Perhaps you have an experienced mentor to whom you can go, or colleagues who will be supportive. Alternatively, and this tends to be my own approach, you can take your ideas to someone who is involved in the area of the inquiry but who might have an alternative perspective to you. This conversation then becomes a further element of your information gathering.

Selecting what information is significant

Imagine you have an important meeting with a senior manager at a large company. Getting his support is crucial to your project for a community centre. As you enter his large office, you notice the flowers on a side table and a photograph of him, smiling happily, standing beside a woman of an apparently different ethnic group. You also notice large piles of papers on his desk and a stream of people coming and going to and from the office, delaying the start to your own conversation. The senior manager appears to give each of the questions asked of him consideration but his manner is brusque and he seems irritated by the constant demands on him. Finally he turns to you, offering you a thin smile that doesn't really change your sense that this has not been a good day for him.

Now, all of the above is information that you've gathered from your observation of what has been going on in that office; but which pieces of information are significant to your own particular project for the community centre? Well, I won't spend too long on this point, but I would suggest that the vase of flowers is not very important, while the fact that he seems irritated and busy might be significant in encouraging you to make your requests briskly and not hold this man up too long. I think that I'd fear that delaying him would not do your project much good.

All right, the example above is one of those instant assessments that we make daily in our lives, but it does illustrate a key process that will go on in any productive inquiry that we undertake. Hopefully, we will usually have a little more time to consider and weigh up our judgements and actions. So, how do we go about making judgements about what is significant to our inquiry project?

Coding

Qualitative researchers have developed a technique from grounded theory called coding that will help us at this stage in our productive inquiry. Coding is a process of categorising the information that we have gathered, and dividing up comments, observations, artefacts and documents into different groups, so that in some way we can say that each category contains material that is similar to other items in that category and different from those in other categories. The process of coding involves two steps.

First, you are looking out for:

(a) patterns in your information

(b) perhaps certain words, actions or symbols that keep cropping up; or

(c) different types of people who seem to talk in different ways; or

(d) particular values which appear to underlie the way people act.

Second, you give each category a label to help you identify the similarities and dissimilarities between your categories. I like Pidgeon and Henwood's (1996) description of coding which they suggest involves identifying 'categories, concepts or labels' that help 'account for what is of importance' to the inquirer.

So, in the process of coding, you will be selecting and sorting those bits of information that appear to be significant to your inquiry. There is an important point here, however. Do not throw away information that does not, initially, make it into your first set of coding. Remember my earlier point that the sense you make of your gathered information is (a) always partial and (b) emergent. You may well find that bits of information you don't initially think important become so later in your inquiry. Coding is a very transitory process; you will find yourself coding, re-coding and then re-coding again as you test out ideas and find that either they're robust or that they don't stand up to further investigation and testing. We will need to think some more about this but first, let's look at an example together.

The quotation below is taken and modified [1] slightly from a research project that I was involved in a couple of years ago. My colleagues and I were exploring how different companies collaborated in the engineering of components and large engineering assemblies.

Collaboration with XYZ Components

Interviewer

So, have you got an example of where a collaborative relationship has gone bad?

Arthur

… I think that we used XYZ Components back in 1996/97 to do the R84 frame and they performed very well. So then we said right we want you to do the R90 frame as well, so they performed well on there. So then we gave them the R102 frame and now they have got a lot of work and inevitably they had resource constraints and they have got all these projects to work on. So when we then give them the new R90 frame that's about the time where they've got too much work to cope. But they don't respond by either putting more people in to deal with it or by saying no we can't do this project because we are not resourced. They try and accomplish it with the existing resources that they've got, they fail and the result of that failure is that they lose that business. And there then enters a period where they are not given any new business. And gradually as the work load dies off, they become much better at doing things because they don't have very much to do. So if we ask them to do one or two things they do it straight away. But when they had a hundred things to do then they probably wouldn't have done them for months. And so they became a very reactive supplier; just simply because they didn't have much to do. And when they react

---

[1] The modification has been done to protect the anonymity of the companies and people involved. We gave that promise to people in order to get their agreement to be interviewed. I suspect that this was for two reasons. First, people are often nervous of being quoted out of context and being made to feel foolish. Second, and this was important in this interview, there were issues of commercial confidentiality involved.

well, then we view them favourably and we start to give them more business again.

Dave

There's one important thing to remember, which is that you must realize that XYZ Components probably has five customers using their factory.

Arthur

So if we have given them a lot of work the same time as International Engineering or Major Construction Corp. or somebody like that, then inevitably the level of support we get has to be filtered through what is the overall business, the correct business decision for XYZ Components. And I would suggest and it probably needs to come from XYZ Components that if you are an engineering company producing ten thousand units every year and you need something done and there is a International Engineering person standing there who produces 250 thousand units a year, I could hazard a guess which one produces more profit (laughs).

Here we have two engineers talking about another company with whom they had worked on several projects over the years. We'd used a semi-structured interview process and my colleague had recorded the interview and then transcribed what had been said.

Activity 8.1

15 minutes

Can you identify some categories that might be worth further consideration?

Comment

What issues seem to be significant to these engineers? Two points to notice here. First, remember that we were interested in how to build good collaboration between different firms in the engineering supply chain, so we'll be looking for ideas and details that have a bearing on what helped create good collaboration and what hindered it. Also, notice what I said there about 'what seems to be significant to the interviewed engineers'. You may remember that one of the reasons for undertaking less structured interviews is that it allows the respondents greater space to tell us what is on **their** minds.

So what do I notice here? Well, I notice that XYZ Components seem to do better in some **projects** than others. Then I notice that one of the reasons given for poor collaboration is **workload pressure**, which is put down to XYZ having **other customers**. I also notice that **the size** of these customers seems to be significant. Finally, I notice that these engineers suggest that sometimes particular **management decisions** affect collaboration.

Now, a particularly important factor here is how you keep a record of your information and ways that you are making sense of that information. We need to discuss a little about how to keep **field notes**. I've mentioned these before in the chapters on asking questions and other inquiry methods, but they are equally, if not more, important as you make sense of the information you have gathered.

Using field notes in your sensemaking …

So how would we keep the information about collaboration with XYZ Components? Well, to be honest, we did have an advantage here, for we had the time and money to record interviews, then get them transcribed and check and correct those transcriptions. It is unlikely that you will have such advantages for your own productive inquiry in your own work context. If you can get that help, grab it gratefully with both hands, but I've done many inquiries where I haven't had such advantages and it was still possible to keep good field notes. Some hints first of all:

- If at all possible, use a word processing package to keep your field notes. This is because you can use the cut/copy and paste facilities to move, save and copy pieces of information easily. Additionally, most word processing programmes now have word search facilities which can be most helpful if you have a great deal of information.

- Using a spreadsheet can also work and for experienced spreadsheet users gives greater scope for sorting your information into columns and rows, which can be handy for visualising information.

- Of course, using computers may well mean that you have to spend some time typing information from handwritten notes into a computer file. Additionally, you may well want to keep a record of large documents in hard copy or handwritten notes.

- If you don't have a computer or word processing package, then the best option would be some sort of card indexing system, in which you put either a summary of the information or the exact words on a card that you then colour-code according to what categories you are using. Alternatively, you sort the cards into categories and if one particular piece of information fits into two categories, then you replicate it.

... and how this helps with coding

Let's go back to that interview extract and take a look at three of the categories that I identified to see how we could use extracts of the interview to illustrate the process of coding.

Projects

Arthur:

'I think that we used XYZ Components back in 1996/97 to do the R84 frame and they performed very well'

'then we gave them the R102 frame'

'when we then give them the new R90 frame'

Workload pressures

Arthur:

'So then we gave them the R102 frame and now they have got a lot of work and inevitably they had resource constraints and they have got all these projects to work on'

'So when we then give them the new R90 frame that's about the time where they've got too much work to cope. But they don't respond by either putting more people in to deal with it or by saying no we can't do this project because we are not resourced.'

'And there then enters a period where they are not given any new business. And gradually as the workload dies off, they become much better at doing things because they don't have very much to do. So if we ask them to do one or two things and they do it straight away.'

Other customers (size)

Dave:

'There's one important thing to remember, which is that you must realize that XYZ Components probably has five customers using their factory.'

Arthur:

'So if we have given them a lot of work the same time as International Engineering or Major Construction Corp. or somebody like that, then inevitably the level of support we get has to be filtered through what is the overall business'

'that if you are an engineering company producing ten thousand units every year and you need something done and there is a International Engineering person standing there who produces 250 thousand units a year, I could hazard a guess which one produces more profit (laughs)'

Note the way that I've cut and pasted whole sentences for the most part, so that I can remember a little of the context of the quotation. Another technique that can help, if you are able to transcribe full interviews, is to number the lines of the interviews, so that you can find extracts in the full interview again quickly. However, my suspicion is that during a productive inquiry within your work context that will be unlikely, and your cards or your computer files will contain extracts of interviews such as my example above.

Two other techniques for managing your field notes might come in handy. First, especially if you are keeping records on a computer, do use keywords to help you remember and find pieces of information. This is particularly helpful when you start to review your thinking and compare your ideas across a wide array of material.

A second technique may help, especially if you do not have frequent access to a computer or if the bulk of your gathered information is not in a form (such as letters, reports or handwritten notes) that can easily be fitted into a computer file. The technique is called **three-column analysis**.

Three-column analysis

As the name implies, this is a method for writing up field notes that splits your writing into three columns. I found it helpful during my own masters' project.

Information	*Sensemaking*	*Meetings*
In this column you can write down details of information that you come across. Of course, sometimes this will just be a note that refers you elsewhere for the full data, but you can still jot down the important details.	Information or records without analysis or interpretation are not worth anything. What does this information mean to your project, your working relationships, your plans? This second column will allow you to ponder these issues and put your thoughts into words. Where are you up to? What do you need to do next, and why? What did so and so mean when she said '....'? All these questions can be ruminated upon in the sensemaking column.	Or you could call this column 'actions', whichever helps you. But in this column you can keep a record of the meetings that are important. You could include details such as the date, who was there and what was said that was significant. Of course, that last question will take you back into the analysis column.

In setting things out, you might want to make the 'sensemaking' column larger than the other two, as I suspect that you will write more in it.

You will find a flow developing. Information will lead to sensemaking, which may well lead to the need to discuss a point with someone, or some people, which will, in turn, require you to do more sensemaking, and so on. One thing that I've always found helpful is to actually put in arrows that show me how my thinking is moving into actions and conversations. A while ago, I sketched out the example in Figure 8.2 in answer to a student who asked what a three-column analysis looked like.

Information	Sensemaking	Meetings
		28/3: phone call from Paul during which we discussed grounded theory and methods for keeping a record of work done on the project. I suggested 3-column analysis and said that I'd get back to him.
	Golly! Can I remember how I did it? I've got some records in my office, and I placed my analysis in the appendix of my own MBA project.	
Found project and saw that the three column headings were: Information, Sensemaking and Meetings.		
	How can I best introduce Paul to this analysis so that it is meaningful? And might other students find this tool useful? I guess that doing a worked example of how I decided to do this paper might make things easier than just a description.	
		PM 28/3: Attach this onto an email to Paul and post it on the website

Figure 8.2 Example of a three-column analysis

Interpreting the information you've gathered

Category definition and theoretical memos

Once you've done your initial coding it's worth spending some time reading through your different categories and writing a brief definition of each. This really doesn't need to be a long essay; just a couple of lines will help you with the next stage of your inquiry when you re-examine the categories and will help you notice how robust your categories are.

At the same time as you are writing these definitions you can also start writing yourself 'memos' in which you start to theorise about why things are happening as they are. These memos need not be long; I suspect that mine are rarely more than half a side of A4 paper. The point is to jot down (I tend to type[2]) how you are making sense of what is going on. Comment on points that interest you, relationships that seem significant, ideas as to why things happen as they do. The reason that writing these thoughts down is helpful is because you can then revisit them and review whether they make sense as you do further thinking and inquiring. Perhaps most importantly, these memos can become the basis of your next cycle of inquiry as you test the value of these initial thoughts. In a few paragraphs' time, I will give an example of how I used a memo in this way during my project with Premier Engineering.

Constant comparison method

One grounded theory approach by which the strength and usefulness of your categories is assessed is called the constant comparison method. You have set up your initial codes and categories; now you revisit the material and re-assess how you have coded it. You look for **similarities** and **dissimilarities** in the material. Sometimes bits and pieces of information appear to fit within one category, but on further reading you notice that there are also dissimilarities. This would mean either that a new category is needed, that a current category is shown to be unhelpful or that a piece of information actually belongs in a different category.

If you were an academic researcher using grounded theory as your research methodology, this process of constant comparison would go on, with you revisiting your gathered information time and time again.

---

[2] Can I encourage you to learn to touch type? It did not take me too long to learn using a computer program. I'm not a great typist, but I find it so helpful when I'm trying 'to think onto paper'.

In such a research project, you would find yourself creating and then re-creating categories, splitting them into new sub-categories and refining your definitions of categories until you reached a point called 'theoretical saturation'. That is the point where the revisiting of your inquiry material yields no new insights or categories or explanations for what has been going on. However, if you are involved in a productive inquiry within your work context, then it is likely that the time needed to undertake such a thorough analysis is a luxury that you can ill afford. So, how can you use some (or all) of these inquiry methods without getting lost in a mass of paper and analysis paralysis?

Well, let's go back to that extract from the interview we've discussed above. Remember, what we were interested in was how to improve collaboration between companies in this engineering supply chain. As my colleagues and I first started to look at this information, there did seem to be interesting differences between design projects. Initially, we wondered if this might be a fruitful line of inquiry; what might be the differences in management style or, perhaps, personnel between the projects? However, I continued my constant comparison process and I came across the following quotation:

> *we would expect* them to be technically competent and to meet all of the targets that we have set out and *we would expect* them to have engineers in here to resolve any issues on the ground. *We would expect* dedicated program support. Then *we would expect* them to have enough resources internally to cope with the workload requirements … *we would expect* them to find it from somewhere and provide it.

Notice that I've added italics to the quotation; obviously, these weren't there in the spoken interview but I have used them as part of my own interpretation. Now, just before I read this quotation I had just started a new category called 'us and them' and this quotation seemed to me to typify an extreme case. I sensed that these engineers had not moved from competitive relations with their suppliers, in which the buyer called the tune and demanded that the supplier did all that was required of them. I now had a new line of inquiry: how did the engineering company manage cross-boundary relations? As I looked at our gathered information, the 'us and them' category started to become larger, so that I then split that category into two: 'us and them – internal relations' and 'us and them – external relations'.

Making judgements

Now we come to a key point within a productive inquiry. It is a point where you have to make a judgement about what to do next. Actually, you will find that you're making this kind of judgement all the time, almost without noticing it. Essentially, you have a choice of two different lines of inquiry – take a look back at Figure 8.1 to see how these two routes fit into the overall process of sensemaking.

- Do I seek out further information, through a process called **theoretical sampling**? Or,

- Do I take action and so undertake another **cycle of inquiry**?

Seeking further information

Theoretical sampling

Grounded theorists will constantly articulate their emerging theories of what is going on in a 'memo'. This is a short piece of writing that describes how they are currently thinking about a particular issue within their research. They can then ask the question, 'How can I confirm or refute this theorising?' An example of this process arose when I was working with Premier Engineering. I was starting to come to a judgement about where I might be able to help my colleagues in the company, so I wrote myself a short memo where I described what I was thinking and why I was beginning to think that way. As I re-read the 'memo', I asked myself how I could test my understanding of the situation. I decided to show the memo to several colleagues who had longer experience of working with Premier than I had, and I took the opportunity to have two or three informal conversations with managers at the company itself. I asked if they recognised the issues that I was recounting; did they make sense to them? With one or two small modifications, I was able to confirm my emerging ideas and take them on to the next stage of action.

In Chapter 7, I mentioned the value of using multiple methods (triangulation) in an inquiry project. The idea, I suggested, is that if we use different methods to ask the same, or similar, questions then we are likely to be able to 'see' the situation from different perspectives and so perhaps in a richer way. Some examples of triangulation might include:

- You've observed a meeting at which you think that a senior manager has implicitly backed your plan of action. After the meeting you check up your understanding with others who were present.

- In an interview, a colleague explains how they chair meetings. You ask if you could attend the next meeting to observe how things go.

- A sales manager explains that a new product is looking very promising. You look at the sales figures for the next three months to see if the sales trends bear out her judgement.

Activity 8.2

20 minutes

Think of any situation at work or in a social context. Write a description of this situation. Be careful to show what evidence there is to back up your description and be clear about how you came upon that evidence. Now ask yourself what different way of gathering information might either confirm or question your current understanding.

Comment

The important point here is to keep looking for slightly different ways of gathering the information. That might include asking different people or looking for information in different ways. Do seek to use the full range of inquiry methods that we've discussed previously.

Looking for negatives

It is very possible to get fixed in a particular way of thinking and for that way of thinking to blind us to alternative ways of seeing the world. For example, I find proofreading my writing very difficult. I can mss out words or letters but because I know what I meant to say, my 'mind' reads the mssing word or letter and I don't notice my error. A similar thing can happen to us when we're looking at information: we can miss some crucial pieces of evidence that contradict our emerging sense of what is going on[3]. One method used by both ethnographers and grounded theorists to handle this problem is to consciously look for pieces of evidence in our field notes that contradict our current view and so give ourselves the opportunity to re-appraise our judgement.

Taking action

Cycles of inquiry

One of the obvious ways of testing our emerging sense of what is going on is to take action. This is the cycle of inquiry process that lies at the heart of any practice-centred inquiry. As you make sense of your work

[3] By the way, did you notice the missing letters in the previous sentence?

context and start to assess what actions you could take to improve the situation, then you will be faced with the opportunity for testing your current assessment of the situation in action. For example, if, having considered some recent meetings, you come to the conclusion that your colleagues will back you in an attempt to move the office around, then actually taking the decision to move the desks to new positions will pretty quickly confirm or disabuse you of your assessment of their support! Of course, taking action can be risky. Working with managers recently, I've coined an expression about our needing to be 'tentatively assertive'. By this I mean that we need to look for ways of taking action that will not 'burn our bridges', so to speak.

Back to Premier Engineering

You will remember that I was now facing a decision whether to focus our inquiry on how Premier collaborated with its suppliers or a new, emerging category of inquiry: how they managed relations across organisational boundaries, not only the boundaries between them and other companies but also internal boundaries, between departments, factories and functions. So which line of inquiry was I to follow? Well, three considerations influenced my judgement:

1 I sought to test my emerging sense of what were important issues by looking at a group of interviews that had been conducted by another colleague in relation to a particular design project. I wondered if these interviews, which were not about collaboration, would reveal inter-company relations as being important to this group of engineers.

2 I wrote a theoretical memo where I outlined a new line of inquiry that focused on the way the engineers at Premier talked. I outlined how I thought certain 'conversational styles' were harmful to their strategic and design plans. I then showed this memo to a range of colleagues who had experience of working for Premier Engineering, and some senior managers at Premier.

3 I sat down with a trusted colleague and discussed which line of inquiry would give us the best chance of helping Premier Engineering improve their design process.

Activity 8.3

Re-read the three considerations outlined above and jot down which of the different sensemaking processes I used.

Comment

The action in (1) involved two of the methods. First, I was looking for negative evidence; that is, evidence that collaboration was going well. Second, I wanted to check out whether in interviews that weren't focused on collaboration our respondents mentioned it as an issue. In a way, this was a piece of triangulation, although it was using interview material again; the interviews were by a different colleague and essentially about a different topic.

In action (2), I was writing a theoretical memo and then using theoretical sampling to check – with people who I knew would have experience of Premier's way of working – whether my emerging sensemaking was heading in a direction that they recognised and thought worth our acting upon.

I shall discuss action (3) in the next section.

Productive inquiry is about taking action

The final point that shaped our next action was the question about which line of inquiry might have the most beneficial effect for Premier. I have no doubt that inquiring further into the inter-company collaboration could have produced some really interesting ideas, but as we discussed what we could achieve, my colleagues and I were concerned that we could not see how we could create any helpful action. The issues involved in Premier's purchasing policy were just not within our scope to affect; it was a headquarters' policy decision and we did not think that we could have an impact on that. We did, however, think that we could design new ways to help inter-departmental conversations. We therefore headed off into a cycle of inquiry where I designed a new workshop to help Premier engineers plan for important co-ordination events.

This final point is crucial to a productive inquiry. You are not just looking for facts and theories so that you can understand what's going on better. Rather, you are seeking to improve a situation – to take action – and this will shape your judgements on the inquiry methods you use and the time you allocate to making sense of the information you've gathered.

Testing and evaluating the consequences of action

The final step in the model we saw in Figure 8.1 is the process of testing and evaluating the consequences of action. In a way, this takes us straight back to the start of Chapter 6, for we will use those same methods of inquiry to conduct this next stage of the cycle. The point that I want to make here, however, is that the action we take is a part of our interpretation, a part of our building an understanding of how our action affects our work context. In a very obvious way, any mistakes we have made in our inquiry and any flaws in our consequent sensemaking are very likely to show up as we take action. We will not get the outcomes we intended, and colleagues, friends or customers will not appreciate what we are doing. Testing and evaluating what happened will enable us to reconsider our understanding of what is going on in our work context and so enrich the sensemaking process that is so crucial to a productive inquiry.

Some concluding thoughts

I am conscious, at the end of this chapter that it takes much longer to write about the sensemaking process than it actually takes to do it. I wonder if, as you read, you occasionally feared that you wouldn't have the time to do anything if you had to do all this detailed analysis every time you acted at work or in your social life. There are two points to make here. First, yes, some aspects of our life are important enough to spend time thinking long and hard about what to do and I'm not convinced that we always put enough effort into thinking about the consequences of our actions. Second, we do live at a terrific speed in our daily working and social lives. And it is here that I think that the action research cycle of inquiry becomes so important. If nothing else, I hope that these three chapters sensitise you to the subtlety involved in acting in our world by designing cycles of inquiry that (a) allow you to act in a timely manner and (b) enable you to consider whether your actions are having a significant and beneficial impact on the quality of your work.

Conducting cycles of inquiry and using some of the methods that I've highlighted will not involve you in gathering huge amounts of information before you act. Rather, you will find yourself in a constant process of gathering information and insight **as you act**. Your actions will often be taken before you have full information, but you can constantly enrich the understanding that prompts your actions. This propensity to action is the major difference between a productive inquiry and conventional, academic research. And it is the taking of action and the use of action as a central part of understanding our social and work life that will enable us to develop the skills of productive inquiry.

Summary

In this chapter we have explored the tricky process of making sense of the information that you have gathered during your inquiry. Two points bear repeating in this summary. First, you should be **reflexive** in your sensemaking – be constantly aware of how your own values, interests and assumptions might be affecting the sense you are making of information. Second, constantly **test** your emerging sense of what is going on. As you start to reach some conclusions, ask yourself how you might be able to test them, either by asking further questions or taking action.

9 Carrying out an ethical and high quality inquiry

Introduction

Several times during our discussions of practice-centred inquiry I have written phrases such as 'there isn't a correct answer here'. As I come to this final chapter, I'm very conscious that I'm going to be saying the same thing time and again. For in this chapter I want to explore two topics. First, I want to discuss the ethical issues involved in undertaking a significant inquiry project and then I will discuss how, if 'there are no right answers', we can still aim to achieve high quality inquiry.

I confess that I approach both topics with a high degree of nervousness for I'm uncertain that I can give you any firm guidance (this will particularly be the case as I deal with ethical questions). Instead, I will seek to think through important issues, explore where researchers have come up with guidance and then discuss where, perhaps, this guidance is less than helpful. In the end, I can only hope to outline the 'terrain', so to speak, and help you to make your own informed and thoughtful decisions.

What does being ethical in our inquiry look like?

At the conclusion of a chapter on the ethics of undertaking qualitative research, Maurice Punch wrote the following:

> I recognize, however, that this area is a swamp and that I have provided no map. Each individual will have to trace his or her own path.
>
> (Source: Punch, 1994, p. 94)

I think I know what he means! It is very, very difficult to start laying down rules to obey, for as soon as you do, exceptions crop up. What I will do, however, is identify the areas we need to think about in terms of conducting an inquiry in an ethical way and see if it is possible to keep to some broad rules drawn from them.

Key issues where 'ethical' judgements will have to be made

Punch (1994) identifies four issues that are most commonly raised in discussions of the ethics of research: harm, consent, deception, and privacy and confidentiality. Now, at first glance you would have thought that it would be possible to identify some straightforward rules that we could all agree on. Let's try:

- In your inquiry, do nothing, and say nothing in your report, that will **harm** the respondents you interview or anyone you observe or quote.

- In your inquiry, make sure that anyone who contributes information gives '**informed consent**' to their words or actions being included in your sensemaking.

- In your inquiry, do not **deceive** anyone.

- In your inquiry, protect the **privacy** of anyone who speaks to you and protect their **confidentiality**.

I can't imagine anyone seriously disagreeing with any of these precepts. But let me tell you four stories from practice-based inquiries that I have conducted and see how I measure up against these four 'rules'.

Harm	A while ago, I was Sales and Marketing Manager of a large company selling clothes. I and my managing director were increasingly aware that the market for one particular item was shrinking. I conducted an inquiry into future market trends. My worst fears were confirmed and we had to reduce our production. One of our two factories closed down; about two hundred people lost their jobs. I really can't claim that my inquiry didn't harm anyone, can I?
Consent	Over the years, a major theme in my research has been how to improve learning in management education. Whilst in some particular cases it was possible to tell students that I was conducting an inquiry (for example, in a project I wrote about in Ramsey, 2004), for the most part it was quite unfeasible to get informed consent from two hundred students in a lecture hall for another inquiry that only really took shape a month or two after the lecture.

Deception	Racking my memory, I can't think of any occasion on which I consciously deceived any participant in an inquiry that I was undertaking. However, I can remember an occasion when I was caught in a conversation with a manager, who gave a very indiscreet description of a colleague, mistaking me for another member of his company rather than a university researcher. How was I to handle this? Should I have interrupted this senior manager to say who I was?
Privacy and confidentiality	Here I can say that I have always made strenuous efforts to protect the anonymity of my respondents and have worked with them to ensure privacy. It hasn't always worked, however! I remember one occasion, when I was interviewing a senior engineer and referred to a particular point of view that had been made to me earlier. I didn't mention any name but my respondent laughed and said, 'Ah, I see you've been talking with …'. Especially when you're working with a small group of people, confidentiality is very difficult to maintain.

So, how do you think that I did on an ethical 'scorecard'? If you were to read longer pieces on research ethics, you'd find some stories of very dubious practices by researchers, but, especially in recent years, these actions would have been taken in the light of some serious thought about what was morally appropriate. In my own stories, I have focused on how tricky it can be to 'keep' to some apparently good rules. In other accounts, however, researchers have described serious dilemmas: where not to deceive might have put somebody's life in peril; where protecting confidentiality could have been understood as protecting criminal behaviour; or where attempting to obtain informed consent would have been pointless and damaged a major research project.

Now, I trust that no one reading this book will find themselves in such perplexing situations, although I wouldn't be surprised if some of you faced dilemmas over commercial issues or problems in personal relations. The simple point here is that whilst most of us would wish to strive to be ethical in our conduct of a productive inquiry, we will face dilemmas to which there are no straightforward, correct answers. We will have to work out our own answer at the time. Having said that, I do think that those original 'rules' that I set up above have a place within our thinking. They do constitute a standard against which our difficult decisions can be made. It is not always possible or even appropriate to keep to such rules in the complex, social world in which productive inquiry occurs, but that doesn't mean that they don't have some value in helping us make ethical decisions.

Some practical pointers to an ethical approach

Finally in this section, I shall pull together some practical points to help you tackle these ethical questions. They've come up at different points as I've discussed inquiry methods, but I'll identify them again here to help your thinking.

- It's always worth answering the question, 'Would I like someone else to treat me the way I'm treating people in this inquiry?'

- Do remember that it's very likely that you'll have to live and/or work with the people involved in your inquiry tomorrow and onwards! It's well worth considering that before you take advantage of someone!

- As I mentioned in the first chapter, making changes to the way we work is nearly always a social process. It will be a very rare productive inquiry indeed that does not require some collaboration with those around us. Here, as in the last point, you might well want to consider whether your actions will encourage or discourage collaborative relations with others involved within your inquiry.

How to do high quality inquiry

I have, on several occasions, said that our gathering and sensemaking of inquiry material will always be subjective; we will never be able to look so objectively at all the data that we could then claim complete accuracy in our analysis. Now, there's a danger lurking in such comments, for it might be assumed that if we can't be sure of getting at the truth, and if there isn't 'one right answer', well, then, anything goes. It is tempting to say, 'If something feels right and suits us, then let's go with it'. Is there no way of making a judgement as to the quality of a practice-centred inquiry? Is there no way of evaluating whether we're on the right or at least a helpful track?

These questions take us right into the heart of some major philosophical debates that have been going on for centuries and which are still the cause of serious disagreement amongst researchers to this day, with little or no certainty that any resolution will be found within my lifetime. It isn't the point of this final, short chapter to go into these debates. Rather, I want to see if I can give you some hints, some questions to ask yourself as you progress with your inquiry, which will enable you to attend to issues of quality. There isn't any step-by-step process that will guarantee 'high quality', but the methods I outline below will help you improve the quality of your inquiries as you gain experience.

I shall discuss quality issues under two headings: first, discussing how high quality work can be identified and achieved in practice; and second, outlining how the quality of scholarship can be assessed in a (probably) written account of practice-centred inquiry.

Quality in practice

There are two keys to developing high quality productive inquiry. The first is the asking of thoughtful, reflexive questions, and the second is the constant cycling through action and reflection that is the hallmark of action research. So we will begin by looking at some questions that you can ask while you conduct your productive inquiry, and we will then look at how action research cycles of inquiry can support your quest for high quality inquiry.

Asking reflexive questions

I referred to Judi Marshall's work on self-reflective inquiry earlier, and I also referred to an article that she's written on the topic called 'Living life as inquiry', which I've included as a reading at the end of this book. In a recent article (Marshall, 2004), she discussed how she attended to quality issues during an inquiry into her own practice as a doctoral research supervisor. Marshall's particular interest in this article was in how such research can be written up. We shall return to a couple of her questions about the writing-up process later, but for now we shall take five of her questions and use them to help us critique and improve our own practice of inquiry. Her questions are:

- *Are my inquiry approaches appropriate to the issues I'm investigating?*
  - 'Do they open my view of the world to reflection, feedback and challenge?' (Source: Marshall, 2004, p. 310)
  - How thorough have I been in my inquiry?
  - Has my practice been sensitive to all the data?

  An interesting point here is Marshall's interest in what she calls elsewhere 'inner arcs of attention', which we considered briefly in Chapter 8. For Marshall, our own feelings, judgements and sensemaking are all relevant pieces of information that can inform an inquiry.

- *How do I judge what information to include or exclude in my sensemaking?*

Information is multi-dimensional, any working context is hugely complex, and there are decisions to be made about which factors are brought to the foreground and which remain in the background.

Marshall is very conscious of the subjective nature of her inquiry, conscious that how and when she decides to 'stop and think', or what issues she considers, are somewhat arbitrary. There's no way around this: there are no natural laws that determine the best time and method for reflection. Rather, what Marshall is encouraging us to consider is how these sensemaking decisions affect our judgement.

- *What kinds of theorising have I engaged in?*
  - What principles have guided my action?
  - Have I pushed my theorising too far?
  - How substantial is my theorising?

Remember, here, that Marshall is a professor writing for a learned journal, so we will have to do some work to apply her thinking to our own work and inquiry context. As you engage in a productive inquiry, and especially as you try out new ideas, it is worth considering where those ideas have come from. Are they contextually relevant? Have you stretched a theory into an area it was never meant to go? As I make sense of gathered information I will also be forming theories of what likely outcomes my actions will have. Do I have evidence upon which to base these theories?

- *How will I know when I've saturated my inquiry?*

  'How do we know when we have inquired enough, reached some sort of saturation? How can we tell whether pausing in inquiry is defensive or appropriate closure?'

  (Source: Marshall, 2004, p. 318)

I've mentioned that there are times within a productive inquiry when you will have to take action. And yet, there is a danger here: it is easy to 'just get on with it' as a way of avoiding difficult questions. We are not automatons; dispassionate, objective robots. Rather, as we undertake a productive inquiry we will often be working in areas where we may be professionally or personally vulnerable. It is not unreasonable to take 'the easy way out' or to pursue our own interests in the face of evidence. It is not unreasonable – but it might damage the quality of our inquiry and so we should try to avoid this happening.

- *How can I work with feedback?*
  - What kinds of feedback can others give us?
  - What kinds of conversations will facilitate helpful feedback?

I've mentioned before, in Chapter 8, that we can use the feedback of others to help us notice times when our own subjectivity might have affected our judgement on information. The same processes of getting feedback from those whose opinions we trust (even, or perhaps especially, if we don't always agree with them) can be helpful in evaluating and improving the quality of our inquiry.

I suspect that as you've read these questions, you will have noticed a similarity with the processes we discussed in relation to the importance of reflexivity in qualitative inquiry. The importance of this kind of reflexivity to the creation of high quality productive inquiry cannot be overstated.

Using cycles of inquiry

There are three features of this iterative process that impact upon the quality of any inquiry.

Developing practice

As you undertake a productive inquiry, you will take action on several occasions. Often this will involve new ways of doing things; you will be trying out new ideas. As you do this, one of three things will occur. You may find that the new practice improves your work context and so it becomes a part of your 'armoury' in doing your work. Alternatively, you may find that, actually, current practices are confirmed as the most appropriate. Finally, the new practice that you try out might not be helpful, but you continue to look for new practices that will help you improve your performance. Whichever of these outcomes accords with your experience, you should be able to see your work or social practice develop and strengthen. In reviewing your inquiry, you should be able to see that the repeated cycles of inquiry have added to a confidence that you are developing and improving your practice.

Fine-tuning practice

Linked to the previous point, as successive cycles of inquiry are conducted, you should find that the nature of the changes you are making to your practice is itself changing. As you try out ideas, you may well find that you identify a method of practice in your work that appears to be helpful but that needs further development or improvement. Perhaps, in trying out an idea in practice, you find yourself having to develop a new skill. This will take time, perhaps several cycles of inquiry, to perfect. The point here is that it is likely that you will find yourself revising and fine-tuning new work and social practices, and this will be evidence that the inquiry is going well. I should raise a note of warning on this point, however, especially if you are undertaking a short inquiry or if you are dealing with some large changes in practice: you may find that you don't have the time to get to this refining process. Even so, in terms of developing high quality inquiry, it will still be worth asking the question, 'Can I see the development of my work practice moving from a phase of innovation to a phase of refinement?' Your answer may well be 'not yet!' and if you can see good reasons for that, well, fine. It's worth emphasising that none of these quality questions is complete in itself. You should use several of them in a constant review of your inquiry.

Emerging consensus

Productive inquiry is nearly always a social process. Any work practice, be it within paid employment or in our social life, is likely to include others. These other people may be collaborators with us in undertaking the practice or they may be beneficiaries (or otherwise) of the practice. Whatever, it should be possible to assess whether or not there is an **emerging consensus** amongst your colleagues, friends or clients as to the value of a sequence of your developing practice. Of course, there is unlikely to be unqualified unanimity of opinion, but is there a broad trend to the views expressed? Are there any examples of others adopting your new methods? Has there been any praise of your new practices?

Quality in presentation

To an extent, this section is most relevant to those reading this book as part of a formal study where they will have to submit an account of their productive inquiry for assessment. However, I would want to stress that the issues I raise here would be equally important if there were no assessed writing or presentation to be done.

Legitimisation and validation

Whitehead and McNiff (2006) suggest that an action researcher seeks legitimacy for their account of what has gone on in their project. By legitimacy, they mean that the researcher's claim to have given an authoritative account has been accepted by a public validation. They go on to argue that this happens in three stages.

Personal validation

> The point of departure in any process of public validation is your own personal conviction of the validity of your own interpretations and explanations.
>
> (Source: Whitehead and McNiff, 2006, p. 103)

They go on to point out that you will need this level of confidence 'if you are to persuade others'. I think that word 'persuade' is helpful here. As you read your account of a productive inquiry, ask yourself if you are persuaded by the evidence you are providing. As you consider future action, are you persuaded that your chosen course is in line with the evidence in the information you have gathered? Notice that this is not the final word but a good starting point from which to move onto Whitehead and McNiff's second level of validation.

Social validation

Whitehead and McNiff locate social validation within a group such as tutorial groups, learning sets, action learning sets or some such supportive group. Such a group will not always accept your account but they will play the role of critical friends, supporting you by enabling you to improve your account and reasoning.

Institutional validation

At one level institutional validation may occur through a university or professional body accrediting your work in some way. However, that is not the only way that an institution can validate your productive inquiry, and perhaps it isn't even the most important way. Your productive inquiry will almost certainly have been carried out within a formal or informal organisation of some sort. These organisations, clubs, informal networks and so on can also validate your inquiry. Another term for this validation could be sustainability. An important question is, do your new practices last beyond your initial inquiry? So, for example, in my work with Premier Engineering, it was significant to me that having initiated a new type of workshop, I was asked back to conduct some workshop leader training, and that some of the managers who attended that training had already run three workshops without me and were planning to take the workshops out to a wider group within the company. Of course, some practice-centred inquiries do not come to a neat ending. Still, the question is worthwhile that asks how that inquiry continues to inform your ongoing practice.

Quality in writing

This final section has been extracted and modified from an article I wrote recently (Ramsey, 2007; you can read the full article, 'Ethno-experiments: creating robust inquiry and futures', in the Readings section).

Relating action and reflection

First, in any account of a productive inquiry, there should be a **transparency of action and reflection**. A simple account of 'what happened' next is less interesting than an account that shows how action led to particular reflections and how those reflections led to further action. In addition, two features of these reflections should be made clear. What was the **evidence** upon which the reflections were based? And **how was that evidence gathered** and analysed? There isn't necessarily a right or wrong way to collect and analyse evidence, but your account should include descriptions of both these processes. A reader should be able to appreciate the logic in your process, even if they disagree with it or if you acknowledge weaknesses in your approach.

Relating theory and practice

Second, there should be some **account of how and where the inquirer obtained new ideas**; the theories or prescriptions that have influenced your actions. Perhaps it is just my position as a university lecturer that makes me hope that there will be some discussion of potentially helpful academic theory and praxis, but even if the new ideas used by an inquirer are not from academic literature, there should be some discussion of where they came from and how they were evaluated and why they were considered worth experimentation. There should almost be a dialogue between new ideas, practice and the practitioner. This is a crucial area where practice-centred inquiry can offer a critique of academic theory as the ideas succeed or fail, as they require modification to fit with local, social and working practices, or as they are rejected as irrelevant to the needs of a particular context. In each of these cases it will be possible to assess the scholarliness involved in the development of practice.

Relating others' accounts

Finally, the social action that I have argued is an unavoidable part of practice and productive inquiry will require that **the account be multi-voiced**. There must be clarity in identifying, even in an individually authored paper or dissertation, where the voices, opinions or judgement of others are being 'heard'. At its simplest, this might mean just the use of another's actual words, but that would be a weak example. A richer text will show how others contributed to the emerging practice in debates or by particular social actions.

Concluding thoughts

This final chapter has considered some of the issues involved in conducting a high quality, productive inquiry. I would include ethical considerations as part of an overall pursuit of high quality inquiry. There is but one final comment to make about how to conduct really good inquiry. Get on and do it. I do hope that this book has been helpful to you in thinking about your own work-based inquiries and I hope that it will prove helpful as you actually undertake those inquiries and try to improve your work practices. But, in the end, the skills of good inquiry are learned and developed rather than explained and taught. There really is only one way to improve your inquiry skills and that is to get underway, make some mistakes and try again, building up your skills in recognising and judging which methods will be most appropriate at any moment. You can't wait, I'm afraid, for that moment when you'll be perfectly prepared for an inquiry. You've just got to get underway!

All the best! I do hope that you learn much and discover the excitement of inquiring into, and so developing, your work practice. It gets me up each morning!

References

Checkland, P. and Scholes, J. (1990) *Soft Systems Methodology in Action*, Chichester, John Wiley and Sons.

Coghlan, D. (2001) 'Insider action research projects: implications for practising managers', *Management Learning*, vol. 32, no. 1, pp. 49–60.

Cook, N. D. S. and Seeley Brown, J. (1999) 'Bridging epistemologies: the generative dance between organizational knowledge and organizational knowing', *Organization Science*, vol. 10, no. 4, pp. 381–400.

Dewey, J. (1938) *Logic – The Theory of Inquiry*, New York, Henry Holt and Company.

Glaser, B. and Strauss, A. (1967) *The Discovery of Grounded Theory*, Chicago, Aldine.

Jasper, M. (2003) *Beginning Reflective Practice*, Cheltenham, Nelson Thornes.

Kolb, D. A. (1984) *Experiential Learning*, Englewood Cliffs, Prentice Hall.

Marshall, J. (1999) 'Living life as inquiry', *Journal of Systemic Practice and Action Research,* vol. 12, no. 2, pp. 155–171.

Marshall, J. (2001) 'Self-reflective inquiry practices' in Reason, P. and Bradbury, H. (eds) *Handbook of Action Research*, London, Sage.

Marshall, J. (2004) 'Living systemic thinking: exploring quality in first-person action research', *Action Research*, vol. 2, no. 3, pp. 305–325.

Nolan, P (2005) 'From First Person Inquiry to Radical Social Action', *Action Research*, vol. 3, no. 3, pp. 297–312.

Pidgeon, N. and Henwood, K. (1996) 'Grounded theory: practical implications' in Richardson, J. T. E. (ed) *Handbook of Qualitative Research Methods for Psychology and the Social Sciences*, Leicester, BPS Books.

Punch, M. (1994) 'Politics and ethics in qualitative research' in Denzin, N. K. and Lincoln, Y. S. (eds) *Handbook of Qualitative Research*, London, Sage.

Ramsey, C. M. (2004) 'Using virtual learning environments to facilitate new learning relationships', *International Journal of Management Education*, vol. 3, no. 2, pp. 31–41.

Ramsey, C. M. (2007) 'Ethno-experiments: creating robust inquiry and futures', *Research in Post-Compulsory Education*, vol. 12, no. 3, pp. 377–390.

Revans, R. W. (1980) *Action Learning: new techniques for management*, London, Blond and Biggs Ltd.

Schön, D. (1983) *The Reflective Practitioner: how professionals think in action*, Aldershot, Avebury.

Watson, T. J. (1994) *In Search of Management*, London, Routledge.

Whitehead, J. and McNiff, J. (2006) *Action Research Living Theory*, London, Sage.

Yes, Prime Minister, BBC television programme, Series 1, Episode 2, 16 January 1986, http://www.yes-minister.com/ypmseas1a.htm (accessed 31 July 2008).

Reading 1: Insider action research projects – implications for practising managers

Coghlan, D. (2001) 'Insider action research projects: implications for practising managers', *Management Learning*, vol. 32, no. 1, pp. 49–60.

Abstract

Managers are increasingly undertaking action research projects in their own organizations. Action research involves opportunistic planned interventions in real time situations and a study of those interventions as they occur, which in turn informs further interventions. Insider action research has its own dynamics, which distinguish it from an external action researcher approach. The manager–researchers are already immersed in the organization and have a preunderstanding from being an actor in the processes being studied. Challenges facing such manager–researchers are that they need to combine their action research role with their regular organizational roles and this role duality can create the potential for role ambiguity and conflict. They need to manage the political dynamics, which involves balancing the organization's formal justification of what it wants in the project with their own tactical personal justification for the project. Manager–researchers' preunderstanding, organizational role and ability to manage organizational politics play an important role in the political process of framing and selecting their action research project. In order that the action research project contribute to the organization's learning, the manager–action researcher engages in interlevel processes engaging individuals, teams, the inter-departmental group and the organization in processes of learning and change. Consideration of these challenges enables manager–action researchers to grasp the opportunities such research projects afford for personal learning, organizational learning and contribution to knowledge.

Managers are increasingly engaging in action research projects in their own organizations. Commonly these projects are undertaken as part of the academic requirements in executive education programmes, such as executive MBA programmes or practitioner doctoral DBS programmes (Gosling and Ashton, 1994; Perry and Zuber-Skerritt, 1994; Coghlan and McDonagh, 1997; Coghlan and Brannick, 2001). Issues of organizational concern, such as systems improvement, organizational learning, the management of change and so on are suitable subjects for action research, since (a) they are real events which must be managed in real time, (b) they provide opportunities for both effective action and learning, and (c) they can contribute to the development of theory of what really goes on in organizations. Riemer (1977) argues that rather than neglecting 'at hand' knowledge or expertise, researchers should turn familiar situations, timely events or special expertise into objects of study. Riemer's proposal for opportunistic research is appropriate for those researching their own organization, and in particular those engaging in action research in their own organization. In this article I will explore some of the key issues which arise when practising managers grasp organizational opportunities to engage in action research projects in their own organizations. As the action research literature tends to take the perspective of the action researcher as an external agent, this exploration of insider action research provides an important contribution to consideration of action research and project-based learning by practising managers (Coghlan and Brannick, 2001).

Managers who undertake action research projects may be located anywhere in their organization's hierarchy. Nuttall (1998) was Head of Site when he undertook his doctoral research. As Krim (1988) was Director of Personnel for Human Resource Development in a city hall he undertook an action inquiry approach to setting up a labour–management participation programme for his PhD. Hierarchical location has undoubted implications for what may be researched and how. Higher-level executives may have more access, especially downward through the hierarchy, but being in a high executive position may exclude them from access to informal and grapevine networks. Middle- or lower-level executives may find upward access difficult and be confined to their function or division.

Action Research

The central tenets of action research can be expressed (Argyris *et al.*, 1985):

1 It involves change experiments on real problems in social systems. It focuses on a particular problem and seeks to provide assistance to the client system.

2 It, like social management more generally, involves iterative cycles of identifying a problem, planning, acting and evaluating.

3   The intended change in an action research project typically involves re-education, a term that refers to changing patterns of thinking and action that are presently well established in individuals and groups. A change intended by change agents is typically at the level of norms and values expressed in action. Effective re-education depends on participation by clients in diagnosis, fact-finding and free choice to engage in new kinds of action.

4   It challenges the status quo from a participative perspective, which is congruent with the requirements of effective re-education.

5   It is intended to contribute simultaneously to basic knowledge in social science and to social action in everyday life. High standards for developing theory and empirically testing propositions organized by theory are not to be sacrificed nor the relation to practice be lost.

Managers who undertake an action research project in and on their own organization do so while being a complete permanent member, by which I mean that the managers want to remain a member within their desired career path when the research is completed. Insider action research has its own dynamics, which distinguish it from an external researcher approach (Coghlan and Brannick, 2001). The researchers are already immersed in the organization and have built up knowledge of the organization from being an actor in the processes being studied (Evered and Louis, 1981). This knowledge comes from the actor engaging in the experiential learning cycles of experiencing, reflecting, conceptualizing and experimenting in real situations (Kolb, 1984; Revans, 1998; Raelin, 2000). There are a number of significant challenges for those managers considering action research in their own organization which I will explore under the following headings: preunderstanding, role duality, and organizational politics.

Preunderstanding

'Preunderstanding refers to such things as people's knowledge, insights and experience before they engage in a research programme' (Gummesson, 2000: 57). The knowledge, insights and experience of the manager–researchers apply, not only to theoretical understanding of organizational dynamics, but also to the lived experience of their own organization. Nielsen and Repstad (1993) outline some examples of such experience and preunderstanding. Managers have knowledge of their organization's everyday life. They know the everyday jargon. They know the legitimate and taboo phenomena of what can be talked about and what cannot. They know what occupies colleagues' minds. They know how the informal organization works and whom to turn to for information and gossip. They know the critical events and what they mean within the organization. They are able to see beyond objectives that are merely window dressing. When they are inquiring they can use the internal jargon and draw on their own experience in asking questions and interviewing, and be able to follow up on replies and so obtain richer data. They are able to participate in discussions or merely observe what is going on without others necessarily being aware of their presence. They can participate freely, without drawing attention to themselves and creating suspicion.

There are also some disadvantages to being close to the data. When action research manager–researchers are interviewing they may assume too much and so not probe as deeply as if they were outsiders or ignorant of the situation. They may think they know the answer and not expose their current thinking to alternative reframing. They may find it difficult to obtain relevant data, because as a member they have to traverse departmental, functional or hierarchical boundaries or because as an insider they may be denied deeper access, which might not be denied an outsider. These pose considerable challenges to the manager–researcher and require rigorous introspection and reflection on experience in order to expose underlying assumptions and unreflected action to continuous testing (Argyris *et al.*, 1985).

Role Duality: Organizational and Researcher Roles

When managers augment their normal organizational membership role with the research enterprise, it can be difficult and awkward, and can become confusing for them. As a result, in trying to sustain a full organizational membership role and the research perspective simultaneously, they are likely to encounter role conflict and find themselves caught between loyalty tugs, behavioural claims and identification dilemmas (Ramirez and Bartunek, 1989; Holian, 1999).

Their involvement in the two roles affects their relationships with fellow organizational members (Adler and Adler, 1987). The new dimension of their relationship to fellow organizational members sets them apart from ordinary members. Their organizational relationships are typically lodged and enmeshed in a network of membership affiliations. These friendships and research ties can vary in character from openness to restrictiveness. Manager–action researchers are likely to find that their associations with various individuals and groups in the setting will influence their relationships with others whom they encounter, affecting the data that can be generated in working with them. Probably the most important issue for manager–action researchers, particularly when they want to remain and progress in the organization, is managing organizational politics.

Managing Organizational Politics

Undertaking an action research project in one's own organization is political and might even be considered subversive. Weinstein (1999) lays out the subversive characteristics of action research. It examines everything. It stresses listening. It emphasizes questioning. It fosters courage. It incites action. It abets reflection and it endorses democratic participation. Any or all of these characteristics may be threatening to existing organizational norms. While action research manager–researchers may see themselves as attempting to generate valid and useful information in order to facilitate free and informed choice so that there will be commitment to those choices in accordance with the theory and practice of action research (Argyris and Schon, 1996), they may find, as Kakabadse (1984) argues, that what constitutes valid information is intensely political.

Accordingly, action research manager–researchers need to be politically astute in deciding to engage in action research, becoming what Buchanan and Badham (1999) call a 'political entrepreneur'. In their view, this role implies a behaviour repertoire of political strategies and tactics and a reflective self-critical perspective on how those political behaviours may be deployed. Buchanan and Boddy (1992) describe the management of the political role in terms of two activities: performing and backstaging. *Performing* involves the public performance role of being active in the change process, building participation for change, and pursuing the change agenda rationally and logically, while backstage activity involves the recruitment and maintenance of support and the reduction of resistance. *Backstaging* comprises skills at intervening in the political and cultural systems, through justifying, influencing and negotiating, defeating opposition and so on. As we have seen, action research manager–researchers have a preunderstanding of the organization's power structures and politics, and are able to work in ways that are in keeping with the political conditions without compromising the project or their own career. Political knowledge was a critical element in Krim's (1988) city hall organization. However, as he points out, his understanding of the informal knowledge-based power structure was inadequate when he underestimated the connection power of one particular individual whom he tried to replace. That person was able to muster considerable support to resist Krim's efforts to replace her and severe confrontational conflict ensued.

As action research manager–researchers engage in their project, they need to be prepared to work the political system, which involves balancing the organization's formal justification of what it wants in the project with their own tacit personal justification for political activity. Throughout the project they have to maintain their credibility as an effective driver of change and as an astute political player. The key to this is assessing the power and interests of relevant stakeholders in relation to aspects of the project.

Nuttall (1998) in his reflection on his joint roles of Head of Site and researcher noted the political complexity of requesting subordinates to answer questionnaires that have been distributed by their boss. He concluded that his own participative management style, built up over six years, resulted in a trusting relationship between his subordinates and himself and enabled them to speak freely and provide the information he sought. At the same time, he was aware that he needed to counter the influence of bias, and so he engaged a neutral research assistant to conduct some interviews and then to compare transcripts.

Framing and Selecting the Action Research Project

The interconnectedness of preunderstanding, role duality and organizational politics becomes evident in the process of framing and selecting an action research project in one's own organization. The complexity of issue identification and selection illustrates that the search for an appropriate issue to study is difficult (Coghlan and Brannick, 2001; Coghlan and McDonagh, 1997). How does a manager–researcher get a sense of the range of possible issues that may be addressed? Not every issue will volunteer itself automatically for attention. While acknowledging the existence of a wide and diverse range of issues it is important to understand that any issue once selected for attention may be embedded in a set of related issues (Beckhard and Harris, 1987). Manager–researchers are then confronted with choices concerning boundaries and are obliged to decide what can be achieved within the time and resources available.

Thinking in terms of issues, rather than problems or opportunities, which warrant attention is vital as language and labels are of the utmost importance at the outset (Dutton et al., 1983; Cooperrider and Srivastva, 1987). For example, framing proposed research initiatives in the context of addressing problems or opportunities carries some inherent risks. Framing an issue as a problem may influence who gets involved in problem resolution. It may be that organizational members embrace problems with a sense of loss, wondering about the organization's ability to reach a satisfactory resolution and often preferring to remain somewhat detached and uncommitted. Using the word 'problem' as distinct from 'opportunity' may also lead to convergent thinking (Dutton *et al.*, 1983). The mental effort expended on problem resolution may restrict the range of alternatives considered blinding organizational members to the possible existence of novel solutions. In a similar vein the use of the label 'opportunity' may lead to divergent thinking as this label has a greater sense of gain associated with it. Organizational members may feel a sense of excitement about tackling a significant opportunity that may have the potential for creativity.

Language and labels are important as they have the potential to influence risk-taking behaviour (Dutton *et al.*, 1983). It may be that thinking in terms of opportunities cultivates a risk-taking culture while thinking in terms of problems cultivates a risk-averse culture. If managers think with an opportunity mindset, then they are less likely to embark on a witch hunt looking for someone to blame—as there is nothing for which to blame them—while the mindset associated with problems embraces the notion of finding a scapegoat. It seems obvious from the above that there is merit in thinking in terms of issues without any attempt to sub-classify such issues in the first instance.

What becomes important then is to uncover the issues that are viewed by organizational members as key issues warranting attention at any point in time. In cases that involve complex organizational change, many of these key issues may initially fall in the category of first-order change (Bartunek and Moch, 1987). As already noted, not all issues are blatantly obvious and it is therefore important for the researcher to get a sense of both the obvious and less obvious. It may be that the obvious is but an outward manifestation of a deeper issue which organizational members are not so willing to embrace publicly. Identification of these deeper issues may point to the need for second-order change. What if the obvious only seems that way due to being ill informed on the nature of the issue at hand? Could it be that the obvious has become so as it embraces the language of dissent and reflects the preoccupations of organizational members with consequences, without ever reflecting on root causes?

Action research manager–researchers need to go with the story as it evolves. They are constantly testing as to whether consensus exists concerning the array of issues that could be addressed (Dutton and Duncan, 1987; Dutton and Jackson, 1987). Such an array may be constructed having considered organizational members' perceptions of key issues. It may embrace a healthy diversity of thinking among organizational members or, alternatively, it may point to significant pockets of conflict in certain issue domains. Change triggers discussion, debate and arguments between people who champion competing ideas and proposals. Such discussion provides useful data and is desirable in order to expose different ideas to public scrutiny and examination (Buchanan and Badham, 1999).

No issue in an organization is context free (Dutton and Ottensmeyer, 1987). Uncovering issues necessitates establishing not only multiple versions of 'the real facts' but also understanding the role history and experience have to play in organizational members' perceptions of these facts. In a similar manner any given issue may be embedded in a system of political behaviour, which it is critical to understand if issue resolution is ever to be negotiated. Krim (1988) reports how he was told that open sharing of information in city hall was dangerous and foolhardy.

The process of identifying issues may be characterized as fluid, dynamic and emergent (Dutton et al., 1983). It is fluid in the sense that it is difficult to establish precise boundaries and when such boundaries are established they are often subject to change. It is dynamic in the sense that the core focus is subject to continuous revision as understanding deepens. It is emergent in the sense that issues appear over time. These key characteristics point to a process which is further characterized by the unfolding nature of interpretation and reinterpretation making extensive use of organizational members' judgements, and revision of judgements based on insights gained from new and existing data, stimuli and perceptions. Ramirez and Bartunek (1989) describe how rumours were spread around the health care organization in order to discredit the action researcher to the effect that she was using the project to set up a position for herself. Krim (1988) was advised by key colleagues that he was not handling power differences very well and given a copy of a pamphlet, 'How to Swim with Sharks', and advised to be more 'shark-like'.

Of immediate importance, then, to manager–researchers is the need to gather and organize these data, stimuli and perceptions of themselves and others. The subsequent sense making process points to the need for them to have good organizational and analytical capabilities. Krim (1988) kept a journal of his reflections and observations, and used his academic supervisors to test them in a safe environment.

Finally, it is important when categorizing issues that each issue is framed in the context of its implicit and explicit assumptions, any known causal relationships, and any predictive judgements concerning the speed of issue resolution (Dutton *et al.*, 1983). Making assumptions explicit aids the resolution process as organizational members develop a shared understanding of the issue being addressed in terms of its history, scope and possible outcomes. Establishing causal relationships helps to place an issue in context by grounding it in organizational reality while simultaneously establishing how organizational members attribute certain outcomes to root causes. Outlining predictive judgements attaches a sense of urgency, or otherwise, to the issue at hand.

Contributing to Organizational Learning

The question then arises, how do the action research projects of individual managers contribute to both the ongoing learning of the organizations in which these manager–researchers work and to the community of organizational scholars? To answer this question we need (a) an inclusive notion of research and (b) an organizational framework that integrates individual and organizational learning.

Traditionally, research addresses the audience of the community of scholars; and applied practical research addresses an outside audience in reports, recommendations and so on. In contrast, in the view of some (Reason and Marshall, 1987; Reason, 1999), all good research communicates with three audiences:

> All good research is *for me*, *for us*, and *for them*: it speaks to three audiences and contributes to each of these three areas of knowing. It is *for them* to the extent that it produces some kind of generalizable ideas and outcomes that elicit the response, 'That's interesting'. It is *for us* to the extent that it responds to concerns for our praxis, is relevant and timely and produces the response, 'That works' from those who are struggling with problems in their field of action. It is *for me* to the extent that the process and

outcomes respond directly to the individual researcher's being-in-the-world, and so elicits the response, 'That's exciting'.

(Reason and Marshall, 1987: 112–13)

Torbert (1998) frames this inclusivity in terms of first, second and third person research.

How then does the action research project of the practising manager contribute to all three forms of research? Clearly first person research is beneficial to the individual manager in terms of personal learning and skill development, though it may not promote the individual's organizational career prospects in the organization (Krim, 1988; Bartunek *et al.*, 1999; Holian, 1999). In terms of second person research, the project is useful to the organization through some forms of first or second order change (Bartunek *et al.*, 2000). In terms of third person action research, it provides valuable experience and rigorous study of what it is really like in organizations (Schein, 1993).

The integration of first and second person research and individual and organizational learning occurs through attention to the levels of aggregation that exist in organizations. These levels describe not only levels of analysis, such as individual, team, interdepartmental group and organization, but interlevel dynamics, such as the impact the individual has on the team and vice versa, the team on other teams, and the organization on individuals, teams and the interdepartmental group and vice versa. Such interlevel dynamics are integral to the nature of organizations as recursive systems (McCaughan and Palmer, 1994), and attention to them is critical to the processes of organizational change and learning (Coghlan, 1996, 1997; Rashford and Coghlan, 1994; Roth, 1996).

First, there is the individual learning and change level for manager–researchers, whereby they attend to their own learning-in-action through their action research project (Raelin, 2000). Yet the individual manager–researchers' own personal learning and change are not sufficient if they aim to effect change in larger and more complex systems than themselves. Typically, the most immediate experience individuals have of an organization is as a member of a team or group. It is through that membership that individuals exercise their role and influence. Hence, the second level of attention is to the dynamics of the teams in which they work and that they utilize in their projects. Such attention involves consideration of content and process issues (Schein, 1999). For a team to learn, its members need to attend and engage in dialogue on such issues as how its members communicate among themselves, solve problems, make decisions and so on (Schein, 1999; Wheelan, 1999).

Yet the research and change process cannot be restricted to learning and change by individuals and teams alone. The learning and change which takes place in individuals and teams needs to be generalized across the interdepartmental group, whereby other teams and units engage in dialogue and negotiation. A critical focus for attention in this regard is the impact of cultural perspectives from different functions on the change process (Schein, 1992). Intergroup dialogue needs to take account of how functional areas in organizations hold different assumptions from and about one another. An interesting development in this regard, which is increasingly becoming a significant action research mechanism, is the role of large group interventions, whereby the whole system gathers in the one room to explore its identity and future direction (Martin, 2001).

Finally, the research project does not stop within the organization. Organizations as open systems have a dynamic two-way relationship with their external environment (Katz and Kahn, 1978). The research process needs to include how the organization is affecting and being affected by, its customers or clients, stakeholders, local community, competitors, wider society and other organizations (Chisholm, 1998).

Viewing organizations through levels of analysis is only one part of the picture. The other part refers to how each of the levels is related to each of the others. There is an essential interlevel element in that each level has a dynamic relationship with each of the others. This relationship is grounded in systems dynamics, whereby the relationship each of the four levels has with the other three is systemic, with feedback loops forming a complex pattern of relationships (McCaughan and Palmer, 1994; Senge, 1990). Dysfunctions at any of the four levels can cause dysfunctions at any of the other three levels. An individual's level of disaffection may be expressed in dysfunctional behaviour in the team and affect a team's ability to function effectively, which in turn reinforces the individual's disaffection. If a team is not functioning effectively, it can limit the interdepartmental group's effectiveness, which may depend on the quality and timeliness of information, resources and partially completed work from that team. If the interdepartmental group's multiple activities are not co-ordinated, the organization's ability to compete effectively may be affected. In systemic terms, each of the four levels affects each of the other three.

For action research manager–researchers, the political dynamics of framing and selecting an action research project, of using their preunderstanding and the action research process to assess the scope of the issue and the degree of political support and/or opposition involve working with individuals, teams, and across the interdepartmental group in order that individual learning can be aggregated into organizational learning (Coghlan, 1997). Such dynamics are critical to bridging the wide gap which exists between individual and organizational learning.

The Value of Insider Action Research for Project-based Learning

In many respects most of the above elements pertain to any work-based project. All managers need to be able to engage in experiential learning or action research, to use their preunderstanding in their managerial role and be able to manage organizational politics. What role, then, does insider action research contribute to project-based learning? There are two elements to an answer to this question.

First, project-based learning demands rigour. Rigour in action research refers to how data are generated, gathered, explored and evaluated, how events are questioned and interpreted through multiple action research cycles (Eden and Huxham, 1996). In other words, action research manager–researchers need to show:

1 how they engaged in the steps of multiple and repetitious action research cycles (how diagnosing, planning, taking action and evaluating were done), and how these were recorded to reflect that they are a true representation of what was studied;

2 how they challenged and tested their own assumptions and interpretations of what was happening continuously through the project by means of public reflection, so that their familiarity with and closeness to the issues are exposed to critique;

3 how they accessed different views of what was happening which probably produced both confirming and contradictory interpretations; and

4 how their interpretations and diagnoses were grounded in scholarly theory, rigorously applied, and how project outcomes were challenged, supported or disconfirmed in terms of the theories underpinning those interpretations and diagnoses.

The value in action research is not whether the project was successful or not, but rather that the exploration of the data, i.e. how a particular project was managed, provides useful and interesting theory which may contribute to learning on the subject of project-based management.

Second, action research consultants or trainers play an important role in ensuring that action research projects generate individual and organizational learning. Through a range of interventions which focus on enabling manager–researchers to engage in inquiry, reflection and theorizing about their project, action research consultants facilitate the enactment of action research cycles on the research project itself. Such interventions typically implement a range of process consultation behaviours, for example exploratory and diagnostic inquiry and confrontation (Schein, 1999; Coghlan and Brannick, 2001).

Conclusions

In this article I have reflected on the opportunities and challenges for managers doing action research projects in and on their own organization, while being a complete permanent member, which in this context means both having insider preunderstanding and access, and wanting to remain a member within a desired career path when the research is completed. This view of action research is rarely afforded much attention (Coghlan and Brannick, 2001).

In considering such insider action research projects, potential manager–researchers need to be aware of the strengths and limits of their preunderstanding, so that they can use their experiential knowledge to reframe their understanding of situations to which they are close. They need to consider the impact of organizational politics on the process of inquiry, who the major players are, and how they can be engaged in the process. Preunderstanding of organizational politics plays an important role in framing and selecting an insider action research project. What appears clear at the outset may lose its apparent clarity as the project unfolds. How the project is framed and subsequently reframed may be a source of important learning. Finally, the ability of individuals' action research projects to have an impact on what and how the organization learns involves strategies of aggregating individual learning to team and interdepartmental group and organizational learning. Consideration of such issues as these enables managers to meet the challenges of doing action research in their own organization, and so provides interesting and exciting research for the development of their organizations.

References

Adler, P. A. and Adler, P. (1987) *Membership Roles in Field Research*. Thousand Oaks, CA: Sage.

Argyris, C., Putnam, R. and Smith, D. (1985) *Action Science*. San Francisco: Jossey-Bass.

Argyris, C. and Schon, D. (1996) *Organizational Learning II*. Reading, MA: Addison-Wesley.

Bartunek, J. M., Crosta, T. E., Dame, R. F. and LeLacheur, D. F. (2000) 'Managers and Project Leaders Conducting their own Action Research Interventions', in R. T. Golembiewski (ed.) *Handbook of Organizational Consultation*, 2nd edn., pp. 59–69. New York: Marcel Dekker.

Bartunek, J. M., Krim, R., Necochea, R. and Humphries, M. (1999) 'Sensemaking, Sensegiving and Leadership in Strategic Organization Development', in J. Wagner III(ed.) *Advances in Qualitative Research*, Vol. 2, pp. 37–71. Greenwich, CT: JAI.

Bartunek, J. M. and Moch, M. K. (1987) 'First-order, Second-order and Third-order Change and Organization Development Interventions: A Cognitive Approach', *Journal of Applied Behavioral Science* 23: 483–500.

Beckhard, R. and Harris, R. (1987) *Organizational Transitions: Managing Complex Change*, 2nd edn. Reading, MA: Addison-Wesley.

Buchanan, D. and Badham, R. (1999) *Power, Politics and Organizational Change: Winning the Turf Game*. London: Sage.

Buchanan, D. and Boddy, D. (1992) *The Expertise of the Change Agent*. London: Prentice Hall.

Chisholm, R. F. (1998) *Developing Network Organizations*. Reading, MA: Addison-Wesley.

Coghlan, D. (1996) 'Mapping the Progress of Change through Organizational Levels: The Example of a Religious Order', in R. Woodman and W. Pasmore (eds) *Research in Organizational Change and Development*, Vol. 9, pp. 123–50. Greenwich, CT: JAI.

Coghlan, D. (1997) 'Organizational Learning as a Dynamic Interlevel Process', in M. A. Rahim, R. T. Golembiewski and L. E. Pate (eds) *Current Topics in Management*, Vol. 2, pp. 27–44. Greenwich, CT: JAI.

Coghlan, D. and Brannick, T. (2001) *Doing Action Research in Your Own Organization*. London: Sage.

Coghlan, D. and McDonagh, J. (1997) 'Doing Action Science in Your Own Organization', in T. Brannick, and W. K. Roche (eds) *Business Research Methods: Strategies, Techniques and Sources*, pp. 139–61. Dublin: Oak Tree Press.

Cooperrider, D. L. and Srivastva, S. (1987) 'Appreciative Inquiry in Organizational Life', in R. Woodman and W. Pasmore (eds) *Research in Organizational Change and Development*, Vol. 1, pp. 129–69. Greenwich, CT: JAI.

Dutton, J. E. and Duncan, R. B. (1987) 'The Creation of Momentum for Change through the Process of Strategic Issue Diagnosis', *Strategic Management Journal* 8: 279–95.

Dutton, J. E., Fahey, L. and Narayanan, V. K. (1983) 'Toward Understanding Strategic Issue Diagnosis', *Strategic Management Journal* 4: 307–23.

Dutton, J. E. and Jackson, S. E. (1987) 'Categorizing Strategic Issues: Links to Organizational Action', *Academy of Management Review* 12(1): 76–90.

Dutton, J. E. and Ottensmeyer, E. (1987) 'Strategic Issues Management Systems: Forms, Functions and Contexts', *Academy of Management Review* 12(2): 355–65.

Eden, C. and Huxham, C. (1996) 'Action Research for Management Research', *British Journal of Management* 7: 75–86.

Evered, M. and Louis, M. R. (1981) 'Alternative Perspectives in the Organizational Sciences: "Inquiry from the Inside" and "Inquiry from the Outside"', *Academy of Management Review* 6: 385–95.

Gosling, J. and Ashton, D. (1994) 'Action Learning and Academic Qualifications', *Management Learning* 25(2): 263–74.

Gummesson, E. (2000) *Qualitative Methods in Management Research*, 2nd edn. Thousand Oaks, CA: Sage.

Holian, R. (1999) 'Doing Action Research in My Own Organization: Ethical Dilemmas, Hopes and Triumphs', *Action Research International*, Paper 3. http://www.scu.edu.au/schools/sawd/ari/ari/holian.html

Kakabadse, A. (1984) 'Politics of a Process Consultant', in A. Kakabadse and C. Parker (eds) *Power, Politics and Organizations*, pp. 169–83. Chichester, UK: Wiley.

Katz, D. and Kahn, R. L. (1978) *The Social Psychology of Organizations*, 2nd edn. New York: McGraw-Hill.

Kolb, D. (1984) *Experiential Learning*. Englewood Cliffs, NJ: Prentice Hall.

Krim, R. (1988) 'Managing to Learn: Action Inquiry in City Hall', in P. Reason (ed.) *Human Inquiry in Action*, pp. 144–62. London: Sage.

McCaughan, N. and Palmer, B. (1994) *Systems Thinking for Harassed Managers*. London: Karnac.

Martin, A. (2001) 'Large Group Processes as Action Research', in P. Reason and H. Bradbury (eds) *Handbook of Action Research*, pp. 200–8. Thousand Oaks, CA: Sage.

Nielsen, J. C. R. and Repstad, P. (1993) 'From Nearness to Distance—and Back: Analyzing Your Own Organization'. Copenhagen Business School, Institute of Organizational and Industrial Sociology, *Papers in Organizations* No. 14.

Nuttall, P. A. (1998) 'Understanding "Empowerment": A Study in a Manufacturing Company', unpublished PhD thesis, Henley Management College and Brunel University, UK.

Perry, C. and Zuber-Skerritt, O. (1994) 'Doctorates by Action Research for Senior Practising Managers', *Management Learning* 25(2): 341–64.

Raelin, J. A. (2000) *Work-Based Learning: The New Frontier of Management Development*. Upper Saddle River, NJ: Prentice Hall.

Ramirez, I. and Bartunek, J. M. (1989) 'The Multiple Realities and Experience of Internal Organization Development Consultation in Health Care', *Journal of Organizational Change Management* 2(1): 40–56.

Rashford, N. S. and Coghlan, D. (1994) *The Dynamics of Organizational Levels: A Change Framework for Managers and Consultants*. Reading, MA: Addison-Wesley.

Reason, P. (1999) 'Integrating Action and Reflection through Co-operative Inquiry', *Management Learning* 30(2): 207–26.

Reason, P. and Marshall, J. (1987) 'Research as Personal Process', in D. Boud and V. Griffin (eds) *Appreciating Adult Learning*, pp. 112–26. London: Kogan Page.

Revans, R. (1998) *ABC of Action Learning*. London: Lemos and Crane.

Riemer, J. (1977) 'Varieties of Opportunistic Research', *Urban Life* 5(4): 467–77.

Roth, G. (1996) 'From Individual and Team Learning to Systems Learning', in S. Cavaleri and D. Fearon (eds) *Managing Organizations that Learn*, pp. 224–45. Cambridge: Blackwell.

Schein, E. H. (1992) *Organizational Culture and Leadership*, 2nd edn. San Francisco: Jossey-Bass.

Schein, E. H. (1993) 'Legitimizing Clinical Research in the Study of Organizational Culture', *Journal of Counseling and Development* 71: 703–8.

Schein, E. H. (1999) *Process Consultation Revisited: Building the Helping Relationship*. Reading, MA: Addison-Wesley.

Senge, P. (1990) *The Fifth Discipline*. New York: Doubleday.

Torbert, W. R. (1998) 'Developing Wisdom and Courage in Organizing and Sciencing', in S. Srivastva and D. L. Cooperrider (eds) *Organizational Wisdom and Executive Courage*, pp. 222–53. San Francisco: New Lexington Press.

Weinstein, K. (1999) *Action Learning: A Practical Guide*, 2nd edn. Aldershot, UK: Gower.

Wheelan, S. A. (1999) *Creating Effective Teams*. Thousand Oaks, CA: Sage.

Reading 2: Living life as inquiry

Marshall, J. (1999) 'Living life as inquiry', *Journal of Systemic Practice and Action Research*, vol. 12, no. 2, pp. 155–171.

In this paper I explain what I mean by *living life as inquiry*, showing how I apply notions of inquiry as method to many areas of my professional and personal activities and how research ideas are generated and tested throughout my life space. The paper has twin tracks which reflect the interwoven processes I am describing and advocating. One is more practice based; in it I outline some of my inquiry practices and dilemmas, and give two examples from my work situation. The second track is more focused on theory, highlighting ideas about systemic analysis, influencing change, relational work, and gender. Writing the paper became an example of my topic. I therefore note features of the text which illustrate processes and practices of inquiry.

1 Introduction

In this paper I shall explore issues to do with *living life as inquiry*. I shall first explain what I mean by this, showing how I apply notions of inquiry as method to many areas of my professional and personal activities (in addition to more formally designated "research") and also how research ideas are generated and tested throughout my life space. I shall outline practices I use to achieve this interwoven living of inquiry, and then give two examples of how I have recently conducted my life in this way in my professional setting. I shall mainly draw on my own experiences, but many discussions with other people looking for effective ways to live/be have informed this writing. (Some of these have been with course participants on the postgraduate action research program at Bath.)

One major purpose of this paper is, then, to articulate and reflect on some of the everyday inquiry practices I have been adopting during recent years, to share some of the delights and dilemmas of living in these ways, and so to invite discussion with people who share such interests.

A second theme of the paper is to articulate the theoretical strands of development which accompany my experiments with practice; these become more prominent in later sections. They are an essential, parallel, cross-referencing path of inquiry; they both inform and are informed by my experience. In this paper I have selected theoretical themes to introduce because, variously, of their associations with my practice, the valuable questions they pose, and their potential for further development. The notion of using systemic analytic frames to inform my behavior pervades the paper. I am also curious about how much influence an individual can have on organizational and other systems, and many of the questions I pursue below relate to this. An allied strand is ideas on "relational practice" (see below), which provide some reference points for understanding and critiquing my practice, and raise questions about how gender influences behavior, its interpretation, and its effectiveness.

Writing this paper has become a minicycle of inquiry in itself, and this has shaped its form, the tones of its different sections, and the coherence (or not) of its storyline. It is therefore an example of *living life as inquiry* (its topic), and I have not neatened out some text features which illustrate the nature of this venture. Two main overlapping trends shape the paper. One is a time progression. Early and middle sections largely focus on reporting the past, later sections look at current concerns and possible future directions. Secondly, the paper brings together the parallel tracks of development noted above, one more centered in practice but informed by and continually informing theory, the other more centered in ideas which are continually cross-referred to experience. It is a key theme of this paper that these life tracks complement and interweave with each other; at times they will be strongly associated and, at others, more weakly attuned. Reporting and reflecting on practice is the stronger voice in this paper. The practice has taken more of my attention recently; it has had an immediacy as I needed to adapt my behavior, and I have used this material as a base for public talks. While the ideas stream has been sufficient to inform practice, so far it is less developed and somewhat piecemeal, and this is apparent in the paper. Influenced by both these trends, the text becomes more loosely connected as it proceeds. I have not tried to disguise this. Instead I have wanted to allow this to be a piece with kalaidoscopic qualities, with elements relating to each other more or less strongly and with a sense of identifying next steps as I close, because that is congruent with, and thus illustrates, my process of *living life as inquiry*.

2 Living life as inquiry

By *living life as inquiry* I mean a range of beliefs, strategies, and ways of behaving which encourage me to treat little as fixed, finished, clear-cut. Rather I have an image of living continually in process, adjusting, seeing what emerges, bringing things into question. This involves, for example, attempting to open to continual question what I know, feel, do and want, and finding ways to engage actively in this questioning and process its stages. It involves seeking to monitor how what I do relates to what I espouse, and to review this explicitly, possibly in collaboration with others, if there seems to be a mismatch. It involves seeking to maintain curiosity, through inner and outer arcs of attention, about what is happening and what part I am playing in creating and sustaining patterns of action, interaction, and nonaction. (Drawing a systemic analysis I might then, for example, explore what is motivating how I keep things the same or how to expand my behavioral and goal flexibility.) It also involves seeking to pay attention to the "stories" I tell about myself and the world and recognizing that these are all constructions, influenced by my purposes and perspectives and by social discourses which shape meanings and values.

If all this sounds like arduous or self-punishing work, that is not my intention or generally my experience. It can be joyless, but that is usually because the inquiry processes have become degenerative in some way—and that, of course, needs "remedial" attention. But mostly this inquiring is a compelling aspect of being inquisitive, curious, and open to testing self and others. Quite often living like this is fun, and has the capacity to turn what might otherwise be daunting, mundane, or duty-full activities into ones which are engaging, interesting, playful, and opportunities for learning. However, I do need to know when not to adopt a thoroughly inquiring approach and to leave life "unprocessed," but deciding when and how to do this is also part of living inquiringly.

One implication of this approach to living is that I adopt the self-reflective and action-oriented "research" approaches I employ in my "work" in any area of my life which seems appropriate. (Surely all researchers have such carryover? But it is something we seldom discuss.) In doing so I am testing out the methods and learning about them in different arenas.

Some of this approach derives from my belief that much research is partly personal process (Marshall, 1984, 1992; Reason and Marshall, 1987), for example, that we draw on our lives and their themes in the topics we choose to study, and my interest in working with this explicitly; I see doing so as good practice. Also, having worked on gender issues for many years, I pay attention to how themes in my research relate to my own life and how my own experiences test and relate to theorizing. For example, as I attend a committee meeting I may well wonder if gendered values and dynamics such as those research participants report (Marshall, 1995) are in play, and whether I am placed differently as a woman (rather than man) in that setting. Rather than speculate, I might then try to find ways to test out the factors of interest, including my own behavioral flexibility. In this integrated life, in which research is not separate or bounded, I *must* hold an attitude of continuing inquiry, as I seek to live with integrity, believing in multiple perspectives rather than one truth, holding visions of a more equal world and hoping to contribute to that practically, not separating off academic knowing from the rest of my activity.

Research is also a "political process" in many ways. Who researches and how; whose experience is researched and how that is named or categorized; what discourses gain currency and hold power; what forms of inquiry and writing are favored by "mainstream" power-holders; and many more are political issues. "Creating knowledge" is political business. Living practice is thus politicized.

My research and values, on gender and other issues, lead me to hope for transformative changes of various sorts (toward more equality, humanity, sustainability, for example) in organizations and society, and I feel I should be making some contribution to these rather than leading the comfortable life afforded by various forms of privilege. This impetus too fuels my need to be inquiring. I have a sense, for example, that collusion with dominant structures and viewpoints is an ever-present challenge for someone working, as I do, from an appreciation of what they consider marginalized experiences. In my case this has often been researching women managers' lives and seeking to speak from and for them. I must take care in my representation of these, partly to avoid making my research participants vulnerable (for a discussion see Marshall, 1995), and partly to help these voices into debate. Many contexts seem to encourage researchers to say less than they believe in order not to breach prevailing "etiquette," shock, disrupt, or invoke resistance. Thus I should be especially wary if I feel comfortable. But also I do not believe in overclear truths, attacking for the sake of it, devaluing the good intents of others, and much more that I might be led into if I saw myself as righteous rebel. Having these concerns is a strong impetus for inquiring—into self and situation. So living in inquiry means continually asking questions such as "Am I colluding?" "What behavior is productive here?" and "Can I contribute to potential change?" And in doing so, it is fundamental to question any sense of self-importance I might hold.

[I note that much of what I have written assumes some notion of people, myself included, as aspiring change agents. I both find this a useful designation and have fundamental questions about its grandiosity and appropriateness. I have decided, however, not to address these questions here; they may be apparent occasionally in qualifying comments.]

Questions about contributing to change are shared by many people I meet. From a variety of roles, these people have been seeking to influence organizations or social settings. Many have now moderated previous hopes of being able to "change the world." People are discussing how difficult this is, are increasingly using systemic analyses to appreciate how interaction patterns are held in place by multiple factors, are more wary of thinking that one person can (or has the right to) make a difference, are more aware of the personal costs (and the inappropriate modeling) of acting largely alone (and under stress) as a change agent in an unwelcoming system, and much more.

Sharing these concerns, I especially welcomed a recent paper by Meyerson and Scully (1995) which addresses related issues. They identify the role of "tempered radicals"—"people who work within mainstream organizations and professions and want also to transform them." They have chosen the designation "tempered" for its multiple meanings. These people seek moderation, they have "become tougher by being alternately heated up and cooled down," and they are angered by incongruities in values and perceived lack of social justice (p. 586). Meyerson and Scully suggest that a wide range of types of people can experience the ambivalence of these roles, of being simultaneously outsider and insider. They look at the characteristics of tempered radicals, especially the advantages and challenges of their ambivalent status, and then outline a range of potential change strategies. Their paper has proved exceedingly popular among people I know who identify themselves as change agents in some way. It captures some of the complexities and conundrums of their lives in ways which mainstream change writing does not.

3 Practices of self-reflection and reflection-in/on-action

In this section I shall illustrate some of the processes of inquiry I use, some dilemmas I encounter, and the resources I draw on, to show the nature of what I do in general terms.

As a researcher, one of my specialisms has been paying attention to processes of self-reflective sense-making, and explicating these in my writing. For example, in Marshall (1995) I articulated how I had constructed women's career stories, illustrating the forms of analysis I used, the issues which arose in doing so, and the negotiations with research participants to achieve a publishable version. Within my own life conduct I am very respectful of my arising ideas and seek to allow their loose connections. I work with these ideas, treating them both lightly and seriously. A key aspect of my inquiry style is to be doing this self-reflective work.

Another element is devising experiments in action (or in relation to qualities of being) which allow issues to be tested. I seek to turn puzzles, problems, and curiosities into cycles of inquiry—meaning evolving processes incorporating appropriate, and repeated, movements between action and reflection—which will allow me to take them further and explore them in practice. Otherwise they may become stagnant or, worse still, turn into repeated mantras of worry. At their best these experiments reap both practical and conceptual rewards. For example, by testing out alternative behavior I may develop ways to operate with interest and apparently increased effectiveness in an environment which previously daunted or diminished me. I may also have learned conceptually about system dynamics and how individuals influence them.

Living life as inquiry means that I hold open the boundary between research and my life generally. Often, therefore, I am aware that a theme I am pursuing in research is also relevant to some other area of my life, and I will seek to work with, rather than suppress, that realization. This can be highly enriching for both my personal and my professional lives, and it can be demanding. I must, for example, accept that life processes have their own sense of timing and necessary resources, and that these may not fit with "academic" time scales. Sometimes I must allow the latter to be put "on hold" for a while, until the former have run their course.

There are therefore boundary issues about how "personal" to be as I articulate my perspective and paths of sense-making, taking these as significant aspects to be accounted in constructivist science (Denzin and Lincoln, 1994). These boundaries are not clear-cut; finding and articulating them is itself an aspect of inquiry (and perhaps any bounded notion of "the personal" is a figment of academic imagination these days). I do not, however, want to tell "confessional tales" to no purpose (but they may sometimes be to valuable purposes) or to make myself or others vulnerable. This is an edge which needs awareness, and when we write from inquiry it requires appropriate signaling.

Images, phrases, concepts, and questions around which I organize my sense of inquiring can arise from a variety of sources, but when they "appear" they can have an intensity which makes me recognize them as powerful, or invest them with such power. They have an evocative quality for me, repeatedly catch my attention, and/or are rich phrases (often with ambiguous or multiple meanings) which echo in different areas of my life. They serve as organizing frames for my self-reflection and for taking issues farther conceptually and in practice. Typically they have been repeated in more than one setting. Sometimes I will be encouraged because they have resonance for other people as well as me, but sometimes this is unimportant. One I use below—knowing when to persist and when to desist—encapsulated themes which came from various sources independently, including my research, my life experience, other authors, and conversations with friends and colleagues.

Typically, when I engage in the kinds of inquiry I am discussing, I notice that my focus of interest and questioning moves on as I sufficiently resolve specific issues. There may be an iterative process in which I cycle through similar themes again, but inquiries which I have lived fully tend to become emptied of energy (which makes detailed note-taking at the time vital for "data" tracking, finer details may not be remembered later). Noticing how particular issues fill and empty of energy is one of the ways that I know I am on the scent of "meaningful" inquiry.

In the practices I am referring to I draw on an eclectic array of resources, some self-generated and some from others' work. Action inquiry as advocated by Torbert, for example, offers some helpful attentional disciplines (Torbert, 1991; Fisher and Torbert, 1995). This model has encouraged me to push more than I had previously done to obtain some response from the outside world, although not always explicitly, and to question my own purposes. A central tenet that whatever happens can be treated as valid information rather than as "error" is sometimes uncomfortable but allows a flexible learning agenda and playfulness.

I also draw on a range of ideas I call systemic (from the works of, e.g., Bateson, 1973; Watzlawick *et al.*, 1974; Meadows, 1991; Senge, 1994) in a shifting blend of analytic frames and approaches to practice which seems highly idiosyncratic. I assume, for example, that systems are highly resilient, that often the more things change the more they stay the same, and that my behavior is potentially system-reinforcing even if I intend it as potentially system-divergent or system-changing. (I also treat myself as a system level with these properties.)

I have been somewhat hesitant about making the inquiry approaches described in these last two sections public. I assume everyone has some sort of "awareness practices" and ways they seek to become continually more effective at what they do and who they hope to be. It seems presumptuous to give mine any sense of status through writing. And yet a key theme for me in *living life as inquiry* is that my learning is enhanced by articulating it to myself, and by opening it to comment by others.

4 Examples of inquiries

In this next section of the paper I will give two examples from the inquiries that I have especially paid attention to in my paid work during the last few years. I do so to show some of the processes of action and reflection I engage in rather than to claim anything momentous about their impacts.

4.1 Speaking at Senate

When I was promoted to Professor a few years ago I became eligible for election to the University's Senate (a major academic decision-making body) as a professorial candidate. I was elected at the next ballot. There were very few women on Senate and the setting was quite formal, with the vice-chancellor and a few other senior people sitting behind a long table on a raised platform and the remaining members of Senate—approximately 30 to 40 people—arranged in rows in front of them. The vice-chancellor chaired the proceedings. I soon became interested in how to speak effectively at Senate, and wondered if my ability to do so would be affected by being a woman in a male-dominated environment. A significant organizational restructuring was being discussed at that time, and so I soon wanted to make contributions. I thus adopted *speaking at Senate* as an inquiry which I made explicit to myself and pursued in conversation with selected colleagues and friends at times. It was fun to do this, as well as significant for me. I also paid attention to connected fields of activity: how I related to other people at the University who were members of Senate or interested in its activities, and how I conducted myself in departmental meetings when Senate-related business was processed.

By making this an explicit inquiry I could play with my own behavior and awareness, and had a frame for treating what happened to myself and others with curiosity. For example, I watched other people's and my own ways of speaking and saw how some are elusive, disguised, easily ignored, or dismissed if potentially contentious. To illustrate, I noticed two comment formats which seemed especially unlikely to lead into further discussion. In one the speakers would make various points showing that they were concerned about or opposed to a suggested course of action and then abruptly stop speaking; they usually did not state the purposes of their comments or suggest how to proceed with them. Typically the discussion simply moved to the next speaker. Or a question would be posed which had the skeleton form (with more words included) of "Surely the vice-chancellor thinks that x is a bad idea?" The vice-chancellor only had to say "no," should he choose to, for any debate to be deflected. In both cases, the issues might be raised again by later speakers, but their initial impetus was usually compromised. I developed and copied alternative forms for making statements of opinion, often saying in what way I intended the comment, and often explicitly inviting a response from the vice-chancellor or fellow senators. Also, I generally avoided making more than two points in one statement, as I found I could not hold a clear "message" while doing so.

I processed this inquiry through my own reflection and self-observation —through anticipating behavior, noting it in the moment, reflecting on it afterward—and through discussions with other people. These processes held much energy at the time, and during some of them I wrote notes which appeared to arrive at insights, to help me ask myself productive questions, to suggest new strategies and ways of behaving, and to give legitimacy to interventions which had sometimes felt awkward or out of place in the setting of the meeting.

As I found I could speak at Senate in ways which maintained my sense of integrity and which also elicited some meaningful engagements, and I became more aware of some (only) of the many other dynamics happening around me, I became more comfortable there and so the early excitement of the inquiry abated (although I will always see this as a sensitive, politicized, environment to be approached somewhat warily, not to be treated as routine). Also, I arrived at more settled formulations of my role in related arenas. One key objective I developed was simply to distribute information to places in the system which it might not otherwise reach (Meadows, 1991). But this is not a straightforward practice. I felt I could sometimes seem, and be, unhelpful to colleagues who were considering how to resolve an issue locally, if I waded in with an account of related Senate discussions. This could deflect their attention, seem to place initiative taking at a higher organizational level, and might look like a power/attention-seeking device on my part.

A significant choice in this inquiry came when my first term of office ended and I had to decide whether to go forward for reelection. Good sense suggested that I should not, to relieve some of the time pressures I was under. But I did, after inquiring consultations with my partner at home and a close colleague. I felt that my curiosity about Senate had not been fully satisfied. Partly I enjoy watching what goes on in this relatively senior decision-making environment (appreciating I am only watching one, more formal, face of such activity). This gives me intrinsic interest and a context for my own activities at the University. As I seek to understand the worlds of women managers in other settings, I also benefit from having some engagements of my own, however minor, to draw on. But also I am pursuing continuing lines of inquiry about change and the potential for change as I puzzle about whether and how individuals can have influence in complex organizational systems. (In my previous 3-year term on Senate I had both moderated and extended my expectations that individuals can have impacts.) These themes interest me personally and professionally; they relate to many of the substantive areas in which I work, such as corporate responsibility (through our M.Sc. in Responsibility and Business Practice), and so persist as concerns. I was one of those reelected to Senate, and valued the apparent feedback that other people had found my contributions of value in some way.

And what became of one of my key opening questions in attending Senate, whether gender is at issue? While women are poorly represented in top posts, gender is not obviously a major factor in the overt dynamics of the meeting. I can see other divisions more prominently, based on persons and positions. Some of the men know each other well, and have long histories together, but differences and tensions appear between them. In my experiments with ways of speaking I was not aware of gender codes as significant. And I realize that gender-associated inequalities may be structured into aspects of our functioning as an organization in ways which are elusive, difficult to pin down.

4.2 Revising our departmental appraisal process

My second example is less focused on my own behavior, but more overtly guided by systemic principles. A few years ago I was asked to help revise the way academic staff appraisal operated in our department. A colleague joined me in this for a while, but then left for other activities. We opted for a review process based initially on wide consultation, and then made strong suggestions for a revised appraisal process (in a memo and follow-up public meeting) using a propose, consult, and adjust-if-necessary approach. The new scheme was designed with systemic principles in mind such as generating feedback (individual and collective) through circuits of information processing, and circulating data where it had not previously been. The process of review itself was also system-testing, seeking to assess how much energy there was for appraisal-related activities and not to go beyond this by creating an elaborate edifice to which no one could be committed. At the same time, we hoped that (because of its systemic design principles) the scheme had the potential to strengthen in the future as meaningful and enjoyable experiences generated further commitment and activity.

One aspect of the revision process to which I paid special attention was keeping people such as the head of department, the University personnel manager, and members of our department involved in what was happening. This was a challenge and at times made me feel like a "runner" between stakeholders with conflicting views and needs. It was especially vital, however, to avoid a potential clash between departmental and central University practices. My activities fortuitously allowed our department to contribute feedback to a significant review of the University's appraisal form which was then being undertaken. The improved form was a very helpful outcome and proved a positive element in our revised scheme, something we could not have expected to achieve at the outset.

Why do I call this *inquiry* work rather than just doing an administrative job? (Is doing so a little "grand"?) I do so because my approach was strongly process and people-centered rather than outcome-based, and I used practices and skills relevant to my researching to achieve administration in this way. My aim was to devise something that would provide information and opportunities for learning as it went along, rather than a blueprint for perfection. I was not attached to "getting it right," rather I was curious about what might be achieved and very willing *both* to make things work for which I was responsible if I could *and* to treat what happened with interest and adaptation. Also, I was experimenting with my own behavior. Now, several years on, we are planning to adjust some details of the department's appraisal process in the light of experience. Again, the notions of systemic patterns and appropriate feedback loops are overt in this rethinking.

The above inquiries are not pursuing grand theoretical themes, but are in-the-situation, and sometimes in-the-minute, important practice questions for me as the person concerned. They do also link to more generic and theoretical issues. In my interwoven living of inquiry these theoretical threads are a parallel track of reflection and echo back to inform and be tested in my practice.

5 Developing theoretical connections

In this section I shall illustrate two of the various paths I adopt when working with ideas. In the first example, I take a theme which arose through both my practice and my more formal research and move between these two arenas to explore it. In the second example, I outline a theoretical framework which has several links to the questions of acting with integrity and effectiveness in organizational settings which have underpinned earlier sections of the paper. The further potential of this framework is noted but not developed. As I pursue ideas in these ways, questions of whether gender, race, or some other form of privilege/inequality is at issue are always background considerations, sometimes moving into more focus if circumstances or theoretical frames support this.

5.1 Curiosity about knowing when to persist and when to desist

I mentioned above in Section 3 how key images or concepts come to organize my thinking and further work. Whether individuals can influence complex systems, and if so how, is a key question which recurs in my work role and personal/professional practice. *Knowing when to persist and when to desist* is a supplementary phrasing which has arisen and become charged with energy and interest for me, and so I shall use it as an organizing image here. It was relevant in both the Senate and the appraisal examples above. It has repeatedly been a question in various arenas of my life during recent years prompting much reflection and experimentation. I have used it explicitly as a prompt for self-questioning and debating with others. It is applicable from the grand scale of whether or not to continue certain activities to more minor, fine-tuning, of how to behave at a given time. It invites me to pay detailed attention to myself and situations, and to experiment. It is a dilemma which resonates with audiences when I talk publically about women managers and acting for change. It is a key skill area for the tempered radical mentioned above (Meyerson and Scully, 1995). In my exploration of this dilemma, it is framed within a systemic sense of the world, for example, involving attention to the dynamics of resilience and potentialities for change (and what persisting and desisting will mean are also crafted within such imagery).

Questions about when to persist and when to desist became well-focused for me through the research I conducted into the career and life choices of women who had reached middle- and senior-level management positions and then left, considered leaving or been forced to leave their jobs (Marshall, 1995). These women's stories are interesting explorations in the fine detail of working with this dilemma. I shall now select briefly from that data to illustrate from a formal research base, moving on to incorporate ideas from my own practice.

One conclusion that I reached from the study of senior managers' decision-making was that some of the women had stayed overly long in environments which were unhealthy for them as they repeatedly adapted their working strategies, seeking to be organizationally effective or to implement significant change programs. Whether to stay or to leave were debates they had had with themselves and others. These dilemmas showed through especially prominently in several cases in which women were change agents in situations which proved exceedingly difficult. Most of the research participants were involved in facilitating organizational change in one form or another and were successful in doing so. These four people had also been successful in previous roles. Their recent stories, however, showed extreme persistence in the face of unpropitious circumstances, and incorporated five interesting, although not wholly common, characteristics.

> The managers and their change initiatives had initially been successful, but then other powerful people mobilized against them and attacked the women managers as figureheads of change.

Senior figures who were advocating change in private did not support the managers in public.

The women became isolated.

They became overcommitted to work, losing other sources of perspective in their lives.

They carried on, not willing to be deterred and disregarding their own safety.

The latter characteristic is especially interesting to me here, because it involved not paying attention to important data on their own perceptions and needs which was simultaneously encouraging them to desist. Discounting these data left them without many other reference points to consult, and limited their abilities to act inquiringly. Disregarding their own safety seemed an intentional or semiintentional choice. One person, a Director of Nursing, for example, was too committed to potential organizational changes to heed her own concerns, to trust her "gut reaction," which was telling her, "Slow down; there's something wrong here." But she also said that she did not want to be "smart" enough not to try for what is sometimes unattainable. She had to be committed to her job and, as an organizational leader, to have thoughts about how the organization could be different, to make her working life worthwhile.

> I wanted to believe in what was happening. It wasn't that important to me to keep my job *per se*, but we were building something, it was important for both patient care and the profession of nursing... (p. 168)

She thought that women are more likely than men to disregard personal safety and push for goals they believe in. The sense of pursuing a wider vision was important.

> So, with any encouragement at all, we [women] will go forward and continue to pursue those goals. I think men are more political than women. We look at what the value is, and I think men look at whether this is going to fly. They're maybe not so committed. (p. 168)

So one potential answer to this section's question, which I would take from my own practice also, is that it may sometimes be appropriate to engage in wholehearted self-sacrifice in order to stand for, and so make possible, changes which require this kind of vision and courage. Alternatively, I would argue that staying in a situation beyond one's capacity for flexibility can be dangerous for both the person concerned and the system. The intending change agent becomes too much part of the system after a time and so loses effectiveness, because innovative moves become difficult to frame. Can we have the awareness and data as we engage in any activity to discriminate and choose between these two strategies? I am interested in developing ways to explore such dilemmas and leave them open to inquiry as I proceed. For example, in memos and meetings about the appraisal scheme I asked whether people wanted the demands of a revised scheme and asked for realistic answers so that I could judge how much energy to devote to the task. People who responded were helpfully frank about what was not working well in the current system. Some people made no contributions to the exercise. But inquiring overtly did not engage as much public process discussion as I had hoped for. So I acted largely on my own judgment and my interpretation of weak signals; my assessment of how much to persist was based on limited data.

Sometimes I will decide to persist in the face of apparent indications to the contrary in order to give the potentialities I am working with an opportunity to be realized. But I will try to make this a deliberate choice rather than let a situation slip into such a pattern (this is one of many bold claims in this paper!) and will try to do this with an attitude of inquiry rather than fixed intent. I will then decide to pay the prices involved in persisting willfully, and may even be able to find ways to reduce these by strategies such as setting a time limit to my activity, or adopting a dual consciousness of pursuing matters whole-heartedly and yet maintaining some inquiring detachment. Also, I will want to learn what does then happen through my persistence, as a comparison for other times when I choose to desist. (And these data feed my general interest in whether individuals can influence complex systems.)

I am enjoying continually questioning when to persist and when to desist, and it is serious work. I think it holds much further challenge and development for me, and part of its value is this succinct formulation of the dilemma which I can use as my own attentional device and in discussions with other people.

5.2 Relational work

I shall now proceed to develop another, more specific, but highly related, theoretical track, starting out by saying how I have chosen this as significant. Having identified such a strand, my approach is then one of puzzling away at different dimensions of it.

Much of what I am reporting as exploration in this paper is work carried on in and through relationships. My solo vision may be an important element, but it is often to no purpose unless it is realized, and modified, in action and reflection that involves others. This is testing and leads me into potentially gender-related territory. I have noticed in two recent "projects," for example, how much I consult with and involve other people, and how much time and energy this takes.

I have therefore been exploring what might underpin this behavior, for example, by noticing what is triggered for me if I consult less. Consultation fits with my values about participation and with beliefs that involvement enhances the quality of thinking and commitment of those involved and the effectiveness of action. I have wondered, however, if my propensity to consult is overdetermined, and whether this is personality-based or related to gender through socialization or gender/power patterns of expectations and "permitted" behaviors. As I question my own motivations and interaction patterns, I am also experimenting (for example, more often acting alone, but usually informing others and allowing redirection if appropriate), and tracking consequences for me and for effectiveness of action in the wider situation.

A theoretical strand which informs me in these reflections is what has come to be called "relational practice" or work. Before I consider a key reference source in this field I want to step back a little and note that seeking to distinguish different sorts of work is an unclear, complex, fraught, and highly political activity. Gender issues are often relevant to how work is defined, conducted, and evaluated. Here I shall focus on only two commonly identified categories of work—task and relationships—because I am interested in the latter rather than a wider potential array. Task work is often defined tautologically, along the lines of helping to achieve the explicit task objective. It is the valued label in most Western, product-oriented, societies, as the preceding sentence shows, so legitimacy is generally claimed for other types of work by "proving" that they contribute to task accomplishment.

Relational work can be defined from a variety of conceptual systems. In early leadership literature a basic distinction was made between structuring, which entailed a concern for task and its accomplishment (see above), and supporting (or "consideration") which involved a concern for people, their development, and maintaining good relationships. The latter provides one slant on relational work. Some sources on management emphasize the importance of politics and informal influential activity as ways of operating—strangely, this is not usually depicted as relational but has a harder, more astute, image. Sometimes women are described as failing to recognize the importance of politics, and as concentrating instead on formal task requirements. Politics is thus sometimes depicted as organizational reality, and as more the territory of men than women. (The juxtaposition of this formulation and that of relational practice which follows is worth more consideration in terms of the gender-associated knowledge politics of naming and valuing.)

Recently, Fletcher (1998) has added a significant contribution to this debate from an overtly feminist position. She draws on theorists such as Gilligan (1982) and Miller (1976), who have affirmed relational models of growth and identity as alternatives to the masculine bias in mainstream psychological theorizing.

> Relational theory suggests that although the prevailing models of adult growth and achievement are based on public sphere characteristics such as separation, individuation, and independence, there exists an alternative model, called growth-in-connection, that is rooted in private sphere characteristics of connection, interdependence, and collectivity.
>
> (Fletcher, 1998, p. 167)

Fletcher uses this base to develop a model of relational practice, which she describes as a feminist reconstruction of work. As part of a larger project in a major high-technology company in the northeastern United States, she set out to discover whether she could find evidence of relational practice and to chart its natures in more detail. She used various data sources, including interviewing and shadowing six of the company's seven female design engineers. Fletcher (1998, p. 169) found evidence of four categories of activities constituting relational practice.

Preserving. Activities associated with task, including preserving the life and well-being of the project.

Mutual empowering. Activities associated with another person. Including intending "to enable or empower others to achieve or to contribute to the project."

Achieving. Activities associated with self. Intended to empower oneself to achieve goals and contribute to the organization's work program.

Creating team. Activities associated with building a collective. This "includes activities intended to construct the social reality of team by creating an environment where positive outcomes of relational interactions can be realized."

Fletcher elaborates more detailed subcategorizations in her paper. She goes on to argue strongly that these relational practices were not valued or considered "real work" within that organizational environment, which favored qualities such as autonomy, self-promotion, individual heroics, tangible outcomes, and short-term results. There was no organizational language in which relational practice could be positively portrayed, and thus "no way of describing the output of some relational activity as an achievement in its own right" (p. 179). The intention of the engineers' behavior was, in fact, misattributed as some personal trait or idiosyncrasy (such as naiveté, powerlessness, or emotional need) rather than as motivated by work effectiveness. While the factors above might affect anyone engaged in relational practice, a further issue related to the social construction of gender. This way of working "got conflated with images of femininity and motherhood ... female engineers felt they were expected to act relationally, to be soft, feminine, helpful, and good listeners" (p. 179).

> It was difficult to articulate a relational way of working as an intentional choice when they sensed that they did not have a choice. (p. 179)

This last conclusion raises important, but familiar, questions for women as they reach more potentially influential positions in organizations.

Fletcher's work has become a reference point in this field, but it is also contested. Its potential to restereotype women with some of their classic associations is one main line of critique. But her theorizing is also welcomed because she seeks to differentiate dimensions within the previously largely devalued, and often diffusely specified, attribution "relational" and to speak for their positive value. These activities may at times be gender-associated, but they are engaged in by women *and* men, including "tempered radicals." I believe they are both much needed in current organizational functioning and under threat given pressures such as speed, slimmed workforces, and increased attention to specifiable outcome measures. These ideas therefore pose valuable theoretical and practice conundrums. In both these realms, a systemic approach seems an important companion perspective, to pose questions about different kinds of effectiveness in relational practice.

6 Further inquiring

As I warned the reader in my Introduction, the theory elements of this paper do not reach conclusions, but are incorporated to illustrate the pursuit of certain types of inquiry. As I draw this exploration to a close, I am again looking to my sense of living in inquiry to reveal where my energy and next steps might be. I am working with and extending the above ideas in various theoretical and practical frames. As I relate them back to my own practice, I experience several conundrums. I believe in the efficacy and ethical value of adopting relational practices, and shall choose to continue to do so. I am also entering a phase of looking afresh at the nature of this work and its consequences. It is highly energy demanding and yet may be seen by others as indirectly connected with effectiveness. It may be long-term work, requiring sustained attention and/or follow-through action to ensure contribution. As Fletcher reports, it can become associated with, and potentially reinforce, gender stereotypes. I wonder if I can pay attention to these questions without making relationships somehow instrumental, because outcome tracking (effectiveness-based) frameworks pull in this direction. I shall strongly resist doing so. I glimpse that one valuable path for me will be to continue the linking of relational practice with systemic analysis and action research approaches as I have done in constructing this paper (while maintaining an awareness of possible gender "interference patterns"). This seems to offer a robust array of complementary and conflicting questions which I plan to incorporate in more formal research and in living inquiringly.

It seems fitting to close with this openness. I find that *living life as inquiry* is a continuing unfolding process. As one theme becomes emptied of energy or develops more of an habitual format of inquiry (as persist/desist has for me), other waves emerge to take its place as fresh edges of questioning. Sometimes engaging with them precedes an appropriate labeling and it takes a while to recognize what is at heart in the inquiry. Sometimes an appropriate phrase acts as an organizing schema that then directs attention. In writing this paper, I have noticed that my inquiry energy is reforming around my interactional practice (and the implications this has for space and time for myself). My next steps will be some gentle noticing about these issues, and in time I shall formulate some action experiments or ways of tracking data to push further into inquiry.

References

Bateson, G. (1973). *Steps to an Ecology of Mind*, Paladin Books, London.

Denzin, N. K., and Lincoln, Y. S. (1994). Introduction: Entering the field of qualitative research. In Denzin, N. K., and Lincoln, Y. S. (eds.), *Handbook of Qualitative Research*, Sage, Thousand Oaks, CA, pp. 1–17.

Fisher, D., and Torbert, W. R. (1995). *Personal and Organizational Transformations: The True Challenge of Continual Quality Improvement*, McGraw-Hill, London.

Fletcher, J. K. (1998). Relational practice: A feminist reconstruction of work. *J. Manage. Inquiry* **7**(2), 163–186.

Gilligan, C. (1982). *In a Different Voice: Psychological Theory and Women's Identity*, Harvard University Press, Cambridge, MA.

Marshall, J. (1984). *Women Managers: Travellers in a Male World*, Wiley, Chichester.

Marshall, J. (1992). Researching women in management as a way of life. *Manage. Educ. Dev.* **23**(3), 281–289.

Marshall, J. (1995). *Women Managers Moving On: Exploring Career and Life Choices*, International Thomson Publishing Europe, London.

Meadows, D. H. (1991). Change is not doom. *Revision* **14**(2), 56–60.

Meyerson, D. E., and Scully, M. A. (1995). Tempered radicalism and the politics of ambivalence and change. *Organiz. Sci.* **6**(5), 585–600.

Miller, J. B. (1976). *Toward a New Psychology of Women*, Penguin, London.

Reason, P., and Marshall, J. (1987). Research as personal process. In Boud, D., and Griffin, V. (eds.), *Appreciating Adult Learning*, Kogan Page, London.

Senge, P. M. (1990). *The Fifth Discipline: The Art and Practice of the Learning Organization*, Doubleday, New York.

Torbert, W. R. (1991). *The Power of Balance: Transforming Self, Society, and Scientific Inquiry*, Sage, Newbury Park, CA.

Watzlawick, P., Weakland, J., and Fisch, R. (1974). *Change: Principles of Problem Formulation and Problem Resolution*, Norton, New York.

Reading 3: Ethno-experiments: creating robust inquiry and futures

Ramsey, C. M. (2007) 'Ethno-experiments: creating robust inquiry and futures', *Research in Post-Compulsory Education*, vol. 12, no. 3, pp. 377–390.

This article introduces a practice-centred inquiry method called an 'ethno-experiment'. The method is built on a social constructionist understanding of practice as a social performance rather than as an individual's act. Additionally, it draws on Garfinkel's early ethnomethodological work and Marshall's self-reflective inquiry to construct a method of inquiry that centres on practice development rather than knowledge output. Having described the conceptual forbears of ethno-experiments and discussed the significant aspects of the practice, the article then examines ethno-experiments using an account of a particular series of these experiments used in work with a major engineering company. Finally, issues of quality in practice and assessment are discussed before it is argued that ethno-experiments provide three benefits to practitioner-inquirers: an enriched dialogue between theory and practice; the robust testing and evaluation of emergent practice; and the development of a scholarship of practice.

Introduction

> The Philosophers have told us about the world, in various ways. The point, of course, is to change it.
>
> (Karl Marx, *The German Ideology*)

My purpose in this article is to outline a method I call 'ethno-experiments' for the study-development-change of practice in both professional and everyday domains.[1] The method of ethno-experimentation emerged as I sought to develop my own practice as a learning facilitator within British higher education (Ramsey, 2003, 2005). I shall also suggest that ethno-experimentation provides a method for developing a scholarship of practice. In using this term 'scholarship of practice', I want to offer a method of inquiry that takes seriously issues of both inquiry in the reflective process *and* consideration of how new ideas might be evaluated and selected as appropriate to activity. In recent conversations, I have been challenged about whether a professional or managerial practitioner would want to be scholarly: 'Aren't they more interested in being practical?' My intention is that in outlining the practice of ethno-experiments, I will illuminate a practice of scholarship that could have a value to practitioners both in professional and personal worlds.

Two premises will shape how I tackle this project. First, I will take seriously a context of students undertaking higher education through some form of work-based learning that will require them to fulfil an identity of 'researcher'. Second, I will use a very particular sense of the word 'practice' that is developed from a social constructionist perspective. While these two premises have been significant in the development of my own academic practice, they should not be read as being exclusive and my hope is that readers from very different perspectives and learning environments will find the idea of ethno-experiments helpful.

Centring practice as a focus of inquiry

I have set myself a target for articulating a method of inquiry that centres on practice as opposed to knowing and knowledge. So, first I need to outline what I mean by 'practice' for it is significantly different to what others might mean by that term. Additionally, I need to explain what I mean by 'centring on practice as opposed to knowing and knowledge'. I shall seek to do these two tasks by outlining three recent, different approaches to practice.

There has been a considerable growth in an academic interest in practices, what has been called a 'practice turn' (Schatzki et al., 2001). Schatzki and his colleagues collected an array of different approaches that all privileged practice as a unit of sociological analysis. While acknowledging the many variants, Schatzki (2001, p. 2) attempted to sum up an overarching conception of practices as 'embodied, materially mediated arrays of human activity'. I shall return to Schatzki's work momentarily, but for now I would like to point out that this approach to practice sees practices as a unit of analysis by which academic researchers can know or understand society better. It is, therefore, and the scholarly approach continues to centre a knowledge output from inquiry, a knowledge about practice and practices.

A second understanding of practice centres on work and the competence needed to work successfully and this is a common theme within work-based learning (Boud & Solomon, 2001). Beckett and Hagar (2002) expressly identify practice with work, although they do emphasise that work includes activities outside conventional paid employment such as domestic responsibilities, institutional involvement and hobbies. Here, the ubiquitous term 'best practice' becomes one goal of practice learning. It is important to emphasise, however, that in most approaches to work-based learning, local context is important to the correct application of a 'best practice'. A 'best practice' would be unlikely to come purely from academic theory, but would likely be developed as a contingent practice similar to Argyris and Schön's (1974) theory in action that suggests that in 'such-and-such' circumstances 'such-and-such' actions are likely to have particular consequences. Here again, despite an emphasis on practice, knowledge can be seen to precede practice. A skilful practitioner is understood as knowing an array of 'best' practices and also able to know a particular working context and so will determine which practice is appropriate to that context.

I want to suggest, however, that an alternative understanding is available, one that offers an understanding of practice, which opens up a rich seam of scholarly and research activity for practitioner-inquirers. Schatzki (2001) pointed to this in his phrase 'embodied … arrays of human activity'. As he went on to note, feminists, in particular, and others argue that practices are not merely the output of particular types of people, but that they *constitute* identities. This is an argument that has been developed by Newman and Holzman (1993, 1997) using the work of Marx and the Russian developmental psychologist Lev Vygotsky (1978).

Newman and Holzman (1993) contrast an understanding of practice as a tool-for-result with practice as a tool-and-result. An example of tool-for-result would be a hammer or pen; both are tools used to achieve some end result, say the fastening of an object or the writing of a letter. Within individualist understandings of agency, where the individual person is posited as an actor creating activity, it makes perfect sense to see practice as the skilled or competent activity undertaken by an individual to achieve a desired result. So, for example, management is treated as the more or less skilful practice of an individual or team and education, nursing or other professions can be understood in a similar way. A key assumption here being that the agent, manager or educator is able to distinguish and isolate (know) a particular situation and result that they are trying to amend and achieve by their practice. However,

Newman and Holzman (1993) point to Leibniz's argument in the seventeenth century that changing one thing changes everything. We do not, they argue, change a particular aspect of any situation, we change the totality. This leads Newman and Holzman to argue that practice is both tool and result. For a practitioner this will mean that as they change the totality of their circumstances, the changed circumstances will, in turn, change them. This is an important shift in the understanding of practice for it means a shift in our understanding of agency within practice.

Commonly, practice literatures understand practice in what might be called 'subject-object relational' terms. Agency is given to an active knowing subject acting upon a passive, knowable object. So, for example, we may consider a carpenter using a hammer to fix a nail in some wood. Our interest is likely to be in whether or not the nail is doing its job of securing that piece of wood. However, if we consider the practice of a manager, then the situation is more complex and a subject-object assumption of practice fails to handle this complexity. Later in this article, I will discuss some work I did with a large company I call 'Premier Engineering'. One story that many engineers and managers told me was that Premier Engineering was a highly authoritarian organisation. The way people tended to manage was through a 'Just do it' approach. As I spoke with engineers and managers at Premier it was clear that they did not find this approach helpful to the complex task of new product development (NPD). Yet, as managers behaved authoritatively, and as that practice was affirmed, so they became more authoritarian. I was told many stories of people who changed when they became managers. There are many reasons given by management theorists for such a change, but my point, here, is that practice changed the practitioner.

Newman and Holzman (1993, 1997) point us toward a treatment of practice as a social performance where agency is accorded to relational processes rather than any individual. Three consequences of this social performance perspective on practice have implications for a practice-centred inquiry. First, it will not be possible to isolate (know) an independent cause and effect. Newman and Holzman argue that any attempt to do so is illusory. Second, if any change is, unavoidably, a change to the totality of our circumstances, then it becomes unhelpful for us to reflect upon past experience, seeking (knowing) theories in the Kolb (1984) or Argyris and Schön (1974) sense that will apply in different circumstances. The implication of activity changing the totality of experience is that practitioners will always be improvising. Finally, the change in the totality of circumstances denies us an ability to predict, based on past experiences, what will happen following our next practice. Consequently, inquiry methods that enable us to know what the circumstances are or identify what practice was best in previous circumstances are not up to the task of supporting day-to-day practice. Practitioners need a different sort of inquiry.

Ethno-experiments: an emerging practice-centred inquiry

Reason (1994) has argued that postmodern approaches, such as the one I have outlined above, tend to be nihilistic. There is certainly a risk that a postmodern critique of modernist scholarship will remain just that; a critique that does not develop alternative practices. However, this need not be the case. What is required is a method of inquiry that does not attend merely to the particular intended change resulting from a particular practice. Rather, as we devise methods of inquiry that centre practice, we need to develop means by which practitioner-inquirers can attend to emergent, new realities. They can then notice: the achievement, or not, of their intended practice goal; the contribution of their practice to the process of totality-changing; the potential of others' actions to promote or constrain future activity; and some evaluation as to whether the changed circumstances (the transitory outcome of practice) are acceptable to participants and other stakeholders, even if they were not what was intended. In this way, the method I am proposing is distinct from those versions of action research and action learning that have developed from either Lewin's (1948) or Revans' (1980) work. In both those approaches, the emphasis was on what practices would achieve a desired, or optimal, result. With ethno-experimentation, the inquirer is attending to the *emerging* circumstances and asking if these are an improvement on what has gone before.

Reason (2006) contrasts two approaches to action research. Drawing on earlier work by Marshall (1984) and Bakan (1996), he identifies agency and communion. Agentic action research celebrates individual autonomy and intention, while communion would emphasise a more participatory view. For Reason, the problem of the more individualistic view of action research is that it tends to ask short-term questions of practical importance to the agent. In doing so, wider questions and problems are ignored and so actions are taken that are dysfunctional to a wider array of community. Ethno-experiments would fit within communion for they emphasise an inquiry into practice that is social rather than the product of an individual agent. Additionally, while ethno-experiments might also create blinkers to a wider ecology of systems, their outcomes are always, consciously, transitory. We could say that the ethno-experimenter is tentatively assertive, seeking to act, but acting in such a way that others' practice will amend and develop.

An example from my work with Premier Engineering may help to explain the above argument. Recently, I was facilitating a workshop of managers and engineers looking at a particular new product design project. The first half of the day had gone particularly well and my colleagues and I were congratulating ourselves and the participants for the quality of ideas generated. A problem was about to hit us, for the ideas and proposals covered just too wide a scope of work for the next stage of the workshop to handle. We found ourselves struggling to handle the complexity of the task. Looking back a few days later, we were able to identify some different facilitation practices that might have helped avoid that situation, but at the time we had to deal with the situation as it arose. Initially, I prompted the participants to group their ideas into similar themes so as to reduce the number and breadth of topics. This action, however, had the unintended consequence of making the action planning stage more difficult for the 'topic teams'. The workshop was again looking precarious! I then sought to reduce the complexity in a different way by asking the participants, working in topic teams, to prioritise their activity over a period of time. Looking at the issues they were facing, what could they realistically achieve before meeting again in four weeks time? This worked for the participants and shaped the conversation in a very different way. I suspect that what I did here is not hugely different to what any facilitator or professional practitioner would do on a daily basis. I attended to what the current situation was, assessed whether I liked what was happening and then sought to act in a way that would improve the situation. What is new, I am suggesting, is that such actions, so often unnoticed and tacit, can be rendered explicit for scholarly consideration: a scholarship of practice.

The term 'ethno-experiment' has two major forebears. First, it has its origins in Garfinkel's (1967) early ethnomethodological work. Garfinkel, as part of a sociology course, got his students to act in culturally surprising ways so that they could explore how people reacted and so highlight the ways that people constituted their social practices in conversation. Ethno-experiments use the idea of *locally* constructed realities as a contrast to much experimental research where experimentally generated results are understood to provide universally valid and replicable data. Additionally, ethno-experiments share Garfinkel's analysis of social practices being socially created. This is in contrast to a more common perspective of seeing social practices as the product of individuals or societal forces. Garfinkel's students were able to see what changed social practices were constructed when they acted in socially unusual ways. In the same way, an ethno-experimenter will be able to attend to an emergent world, as socially constructed, following his or her intervention. For the most part, an ethno-experimenter will not seek to discomfort social contexts in the same way as Garfinkel's interventions. They will, however, consider actions that bear an intention to change the social context and illuminate the new context. An important point here is that an ethno-experiment is an invitation and contribution (Ramsey, 2005) to the *social* production of that new context and should not be considered an act of individual agency.

A second source inquiry practice is Marshall's (1999, 2001) work on self-reflective inquiry. Marshall wrote of conducting an inquiry into her own professional practices as a senior academic in a British university. For example, she conducted cycles of inquiry evaluating the effect of her interventions in management meetings, how they affected the discussions and achieved, or otherwise, her own aims. Ethno-experiments do much the same; constituting, in themselves, cycles of action and reflection, but in using the term 'experiment' they emphasise the social construction of a new reality. Attention is given less to an evaluation of a practitioner's intervention and more to an appreciation of what new reality has been created. In this way, ethno-experiments fall within the frame of transformational action research (Reason & Torbert, 2001), where practical knowing is seen as being 'embodied in the moment-to-moment action of each research/practitioner, in the service of human flourishing' (Reason & Torbert, 2001, p. 7).

The practice of ethno-experiments

The actual practice of ethno-experimentation has emerged over the last five years as I have sought to develop my own professional practice as a teacher (Ramsey, 2003, 2005) and support engineering managers at Premier Engineering to improve the NPD process, an account of which can be found below. In undertaking ethno-experiments, my colleagues and I tried new methods in the classroom or engineering design centre. In doing so, we were not so much inquiring into a situation as performing a new creation, asking if it 'worked for us' and contributed to ways forward that participants considered positive in some way. In the same way as a chemical experiment creates a new substance or gas, so an ethno-experiment creates a new social reality. These ethno-experiments generated social performances of seminar activity (Ramsey, 2005), web-based learning (Ramsey, 2003) or 'Gateway Preparation Workshops' at Premier Engineering. In order to appreciate the consequences of our actions and plan new actions, we would gather evidence in three general areas. First, we gathered evidence as to the context that the participants narrated as relevant. Second, we gathered evidence as to the plausibility of planned actions. Finally, using ethno-experiments, we gathered evidence as to how participants and other stakeholders were appreciating the emergent practice and situation. I shall now expand each of these stages of the inquiry by using an example from work at Premier Engineering undertaken by a university team in collaboration with managers and engineers.

It is an important point that our initial inquiry was not aspiring to a level of accuracy about what was actually the situation at Premier Engineering. Rather, as my colleagues and I spoke with engineers and managers at Premier, we were seeking to get a sense of how they talked about their work, what stories they told and what 'language tools' (Wittgenstein, 1953) they used in telling those stories. In doing this, our main goal was to develop action with which our colleagues in Premier could engage and then develop when the project came to an end. Our goal, therefore, was coordination rather than accuracy. This goal needs some further explanation. I am not arguing, here, that there is no reality that can be accurately researched and described. There are certainly problems in how accurate any research can be in its account of a contextual reality,[2] but that is not an issue that I want to discuss in this article. I do not want to make an ontological or epistemological point. Rather, I am making a strategic point in the carrying out of a practice-centred, in contrast to knowledge output, inquiry. An ethno-experimenter's inquiry is not seeking a knowledge claim as its output, but an emergent practice, co-created with others. Consequently, they will choose to focus less on ontological issues of what was the case or epistemological issues of how they came to know that, rather they will be choosing inquiry methods that develop transitory practice in such a way as to make them available for interrogation, reflection and evaluation.

I would suggest that within a practice context, as opposed to an academic one, time scales will not allow for the kind of thoroughgoing research to achieve some sort of valid truth story. As Shotter (1993, 1996, 2000) points out, social life, including work, is essentially carried out in moment-by-moment relations. These moment-by-moment relations create new realities and a practice-centred inquiry will need to enable practitioner-inquirers to attend to these processes of creation rather than static knowledge claims about circumstances, determinants or causal relations. Instead, an alternative aim would be to gain some insight into how important others will coordinate and collaborate with our initiatives and so co-create the new realities we were seeking to investigate.

The key purpose of an ethno-experiment is to create a new set of circumstances, a new reality. So, for example, in my work on 'teaching' leadership to undergraduates (Ramsey, 2005), colleagues and I experimented with new ways of running classroom seminars, using poems or alternative case studies that lifted ideas of leadership not commonly found in undergraduate organisational behaviour courses. In each case, we set out to change our practice of running seminars. In the same way, in the university team's work with Premier Engineering, we developed through our initial inquiries a set of stories about where current planning and coordination practices within the NPD process at Premier were running into problems. In particular, we focused on discursive practices used and were able to illustrate how these were causing problems and that, we argued, we should attempt to change. The four, unhelpful discursive practices we identified were:

- Talk about collaboration in very strong 'us' and 'them' terms. It would be too strong to say 'us' against 'them', but that would not be very far off the mark.

- Managerial initiatives that tended to be around issues of control, what we called 'process disciplines' or what *ought* to be done. We found far less evidence of support for activities that handled 'judgement calls' in the day-to-day actions, where there were trade-offs between different functions.

- 'It's simple.' Perhaps this is related to the previous point. Interview respondents kept telling us that the work was easy: 'You just do what you're asked, check it and pass it on.' There were several problems we identified with this phrase; not least was that it suggested a simple, linear or sequential process when it was becoming very clear that NPD at Premier was a highly complex, interrelated or 'neural' affair.

- Decisions and integrative work that were done at a senior executive level rather than at a detailed level, and we suspected that 'the devil was in the detail'.

These then were the stories that shaped the university team's thinking about action and we shared these ideas with managers at Premier. A key point for the team was that these managers recognised the issues we were raising and were therefore interested in what actions we thought would make a difference. Our goal, therefore, was to develop, experiment with and evaluate an initiative or initiatives that would help our partners at Premier build new discursive practices and would help them develop new products faster and more efficiently.

The initial ethno-experiment we designed was a workshop that used ideas from Barrett's (1998) work on jazz improvisation and specifically used elements of a meetings technology called 'Team Syntegrity' (Beer, 1990). The objective of this approach, in terms of organisational change, was to reshape the way that participants talked about the NPD process both in terms of the topics they discussed and also in terms of how they framed those conversations. In short, we were hoping to facilitate conversations between participants that handled the relational complexity of NPD, that foregrounded issues of integration and allowed engineers, working at an appropriate level of detail, to make judgement calls and negotiate trade-offs created by those decisions. In terms of an inquiry, we were seeking to create changed realities where we could explore whether these changes in discursive practice created tangible benefits. We also wanted to find if they were accepted as helpful by participants, and started to influence organisational integration and collaboration outside the specific workshops themselves.

Evaluation, reaction and action

We ran a sequence of workshops linked to particular 'gateways' in the Premier NPD process. At the end of each of these events, we asked for feedback from all participants under three headings:

- Three things that were positive about the workshops.
- Three things about the workshop that need improvement.
- One thing that you'll do differently tomorrow.

Additionally, we would have a reflective discussion between the university team and sponsoring managers about the day and, later, we conducted a series of longer interviews with participants who had been at more than one workshop. Finally, about three months after each workshop and in collaboration with managers at Premier, we looked for some tangible evidence that the workshops had made a difference to the particular NPD projects. Now, none of these methods of inquiry were foolproof methods for achieving a highly reliable, objective account of the workshops. The feedback sheets were often completed in a hurry with short statements that were difficult to interpret. There was not enough time to interview as many participants as we would have liked, and the judgements on tangible benefits included expert judgements rather than unambiguous evidence and also proved slow in coming through. These points, which would be weaknesses in knowledge output research, are not necessarily a problem when inquiry is focused on practice. The reason for this is that practice-centred inquiry is an iterative process. Yes, it is possible to draw unhelpful inferences from incomplete evidence; however, these are likely to be caught in further cycles of inquiry. There is a sense in which a practitioner-inquirer uses ethno-experiments in a tentatively assertive manner to test their emerging sense-making. Like co-operative inquiry (Reason, 1999), ethno-experiments involve considerable dialogue between multiple partners and because they are considered as social performances, then others' responses to new experiments will be part of the intervention in the creation of the ethno-experiment.

It is unlikely that ethno-experiments will be complete in a one-off process. Both my earlier studies involving my own teaching practices (Ramsey, 2004, 2005) involved several iterations as I refined and developed those practices. It was the same at Premier Engineering. The initial workshop was a considerable success, with participants keen to repeat the process on other projects. Even so, as the university team read feedback comments and reflected upon their experiences of this first and then later workshops, different aspects changed. For example, my own role as facilitator changed as I learned when to take centre stage and when to keep quiet, giving participants space to talk. Not one of the different stages in the workshop remained unaltered by the team's reflections and feedback comments.

Of particular note is the fact that there were some changes that emerged within the practice itself and for which I am unable to find an evidence trail or planning decision. One example was the emergence of the final session before lunch as an interim plenary session. What is more, my role in this session became increasingly theatrical as I challenged participants to think more widely. Even in hindsight, although I can justify my actions now, I cannot tell you why I changed my actions and words during this session. I can only say, perhaps rather limply, that 'it felt right at the time'. The point I want to make here, however, is that informal conversations with participants and our team reflective conversations often lifted particular moments from these pre-lunch sessions as 'the moment when we got it'. In this way, ethno-experiments gave space for the testing of not only rationally planned actions, but also those that arose out of social processes of the moment. The important point here is that the actions were tested and, if inappropriate, did not survive into future practice.

Quality and assessment of ethno-experiments

Given that I am suggesting ethno-experimentation as a method for undertaking work-based learning within a higher education context, there is a need to consider issues of quality and assessment. I have argued above that ideas of validity common in knowledge output research do not carry the same conviction in a practice-centred inquiry. However, that does not mean there are no ways of assessing the quality of scholarship involved and learning achieved in ethno-experiment-based inquiry. I shall discuss quality issues under two headings. First, discussing how high-quality work can be identified and achieved in practice, and then outlining how quality of scholarship can be assessed in a written (probably) account of ethno-experiments.

Quality in practice

The key to developing a high-quality inquiry using ethno-experiments is the iterative process involved. There are three features of this iterative process that impact upon the quality of the inquiry. First, ethno-experiments involve cycles of inquiry, action followed by reflection leading to new action and so on. Consequently, an ethno-experiment inquirer should be able to see their practice being refined and becoming robust and sustainable. If successive ethno-experiments do not start to create practice that is robust in terms of it being acceptable to partners and delivering desirable outcomes, then something is going wrong in the process and that needs to be considered. Second, and linked to the previous point, as successive ethno-experiments are conducted, the magnitude of changes to practice required between them should diminish, by the end amounting to little more than fine tuning. Here again, if that is not the case, then reflection will need to focus on the actions. Finally, this whole process involves, as I described in discussing my facilitation of the workshops at Premier Engineering, a constant testing of practice. Any practice is put up for inspection and evaluation. In part, an ethno-experiment will be designed to offer the chance to evaluate practice in terms of its social outcome. Although here a rider must be added that, given the social performance involved in practice, it will never be possible to identify clearly either an individual's practice or its discreet effect on circumstances. Consequently, this evaluation will always be partial and enriched by multiple voices, as discussed below.

There are two other indicators of quality to which an ethno-experimenter can attend. Using the social and collaborative nature of a practice inquiry, it should be possible to assess whether or not there is an emerging consensus as to the value of a sequence of ethno-experiments. Of course there is unlikely to be unqualified unanimity of opinion, but is there a broad trend to the views expressed? Finally, there is the question of sustainability. Do the practices last beyond an initial inquiry? So, for example, it is significant to me that following the workshops that I facilitated at Premier Engineering, I was asked back to conduct some facilitator training and I am aware that the participants who attended that training have already run three workshops without me and are planning to take the workshops out to a wider group within the company. Of course, some practice-centred inquiries do not come to a neat ending. For example, my own inquiry into the use of virtual learning environments continues to this day, some five years after the inquiry I initially conducted. Still, the question is worthwhile that asks me how that inquiry is informing my current practice.

Quality in writing (presenting)

For the sake of rhetorical ease, I shall refer only to writing in this section. However, it is worth pointing out that ethno-experiments lend themselves to far more varied and creative presentations of learning than a conventional, individually written report or thesis. The use of video, podcast, blog or wiki would all add to the richness of a presentation. Networking facilities, such as Myspace or Utube, point to ways of collecting and then presenting an account of learning that would greatly add to a scholarly consideration of practice. Whatever the media used, the quality indicators of presentation will be the same. I identify three of these below.

First, in any account of a series of ethno-experiments, there should be transparency of action and reflection. A simple account of 'what happened' next is less interesting than an account that shows how action led to particular reflections and how those reflections led to further action. The reflections should also be clear about two features of reflection. First, what was the evidence upon which the reflections were based and how was that evidence gathered and analysed? There is not necessarily a right or wrong way to collect and analyse evidence, but an account of both these processes should be included. A reader should be able to appreciate the logic in that process, even if they disagree with it or if the author acknowledges weaknesses in their approach.

Secondly, there should be some account of how and where the inquirer obtained new ideas. Perhaps it is just my position as a university lecturer that makes me hope that there will be some discussion of potentially helpful academic theory and praxis, but even if the new ideas used by an inquirer are not from academic literatures there should be some discussion of where ideas for new practice came from and how those ideas were evaluated and considered worth experimentation. There should almost be a dialogue between new ideas and practice and the practitioner. This is a crucial area where ethno-experiments can offer a critique of academic theory as the ideas succeed or fail, as they require modification to fit with local, social and working practices or where they can be rejected as irrelevant to the needs of a particular context. In each of these cases, it will be possible to assess the scholarliness involved in the development of practice.

Finally, the social performance I have argued is an unavoidable part of practice and a practice-centred inquiry will require that the account be multi-voiced. There must be clarity in identifying, even in an individually authored paper or dissertation, where others' voices are being 'heard'. At its simplest, this might mean just the use of another's actual words, but that would be a weak example. A richer text will show how others contributed to the emerging practice in debates or by particular social actions. That our education system favours an individualistic assessment of academic quality should not mean that an inquirer's location within, and appreciation of, social practices is not recorded.

Concluding comments

The practice of ethno-experiments emerged as I sought to develop my own professional practice in a scholarly manner. It owes much to my own social constructionist premises. I found that most of the quantitative and qualitative research literatures contained implicit, or even explicit, assumptions of an alienated researcher who did not affect, and was not affected by, the world they were researching (Alvesson &

Sköldberg, 2000; Newman & Holzman, 1997). Such assumptions did not fit with social constructionist (e.g., Gergen, 1994) premises. For if reality is socially constructed in relational processes and if relational processes continue, then that construction is ongoing. I needed to develop a method that attended to new realities in ongoing creation rather than a current reality already in existence. Additionally, inquiry and reflective methods that focused on individual agency (e.g., Kolb, 1984) did not adequately appreciate the social performance of new reality making. I needed an inquiry method that gave space for a polyphonic, multi-actor agency. So, ethno-experiments emerged within inquiries into my own professional practice, drawing upon an array of existing inquiry methods from ethnography, ethnomethodology, grounded theory and action research. I would, however, want to argue that one does not need to share my own, social constructionist premises for ethno-experiments to be of value.

I will conclude by proposing three benefits ethno-experiments offer to practitioner-inquirers from whatever epistemological or ontological background. First, the use of ethno-experiments can enrich the relationship between academic theory and professional practice. A dialogue of equals is created, as practice and theory become voices speaking to each other, rather than seeking authority over each other. Terms such as 'best practice' that depend upon some warranting body (usually academic because of the need for research-based proof) cease to have any meaning or authority over professional practice in any particular circumstances. For the practice is not authored by an individual applying a 'best' practice, but is authored in a social, momentary performance. Likewise a reliance on common sense or the ideas of experienced practitioners (e.g., Revans, 1980) denies the practitioner a potentially rich contribution from academic literatures.

Secondly, ethno-experiments allow for a regular and robust testing of any emerging practice. I told the story, above, of how I was unable to tell where some of my practices as a facilitator emerged from, other than that they emerged within particular, social moments and conversations. However, those practices were subjected to a robust critique and testing. Did they help or were they unhelpful? Other voices spoke into the development of practice, others were able to say 'do that next time' or 'that got in the way, Caroline'. In this way, we were able to develop, modify and revise practices. Perhaps, most of all, we learned to attend to relational processes within the workshops themselves.

Finally, ethno-experiments provide one way in which to develop a scholarship of practice rather than a scholarship that is applied in practice or scholarship that is just ignored as being irrelevant. New ideas are appreciated, critiqued and synthesised. Practice contexts, social processes and effects are interrogated and evaluated using evidence gained from serious inquiry methods. These are scholarly activities and they take a scholarship of practice out of dusty libraries and locate it at the centre of day-to-day life and work.

Acknowledgements

The author would like to acknowledge the funding provided by Advantage West Midlands (AWM) in support of the research with Premier Engineering. She also wishes to acknowledge the contribution of her colleagues Joy Batchelor and Martina Eberle in that work.

Notes

1 I apologise for the cumbersome nature of the term 'study-development-change', but it points to the important issue that a practice-centred inquiry will inevitably not involve merely a distanced, academic study of a practice, but also that practice being developed and that development will, again inevitably, involve change. For the remainder of this article, I will use the term 'inquiry' to capture these linked activities.

2 See Alvesson and Sköldberg (2000), Gergen (1994) or Reason and Bradbury (2001) for different critiques of modernist research aspirations.

References

Alvesson, M. & Sköldberg, K. (2000) *Reflexive methodology* (London, Sage).

Argyris, C. & Schön, D. (1974) *Theory in practice: Increasing professional practice* (San Francisco, CA, Jossey-Bass).

Bakan, D. (1996) *The duality of human existence: Isolation and communion in Western man* (Boston, MA, Beacon Press).

Barrett, F. (1998) Creativity and improvisation in jazz and organizations: Implications for organizational learning, *Organization Science*, 9, 605–623.

Beckett, D. & Hagar, P. (2002) *Life, work and learning: Practice in postmodernity* (London, Routledge).

Beer, S. (1990) *Beyond dispute: The invention of team syntegrity* (Chichester, John Wiley).

Boud, D. & Solomon, N. (2001) *Work-based Learning: A new higher education?* (Buckingham, Open University Press).

Garfinkel, H. (1967) *Studies in ethnomethodology* (Englewood Cliffs, NJ, Prentice Hall).

Gergen, K. (1994) *Realities and relationships* (Cambridge, MA, Harvard University Press).

Kolb, D. (1984) *Experiential learning* (Englewood Cliffs, NJ, Prentice Hall).

Lewin, K. (1948) *Resolving social conflicts: Selected papers on group dynamics* (New York, Harper & Row).

Marshall, J. (1984) *Women managers: Travellers in a male world* (Chichester, John Wiley).

Marshall, J. (1999) Living life as inquiry, *Systemic Practice and Action Research*, 12(2), 155–171.

Marshall, J. (2001) Self-reflective inquiry practices in: P. Reason & H. Bradbury (eds.) *Handbook of Action Research* (London, Sage).

Newman, F. & Holzman, L. (1993) *Lev Vygotsky: Revolutionary scientist* (London, Routledge).

Newman, F. & Holzman, L. (1997) *The end of knowing* (London, Routledge).

Ramsey, C. (2003) Using virtual learning environments to facilitate new learning relationships, *International Journal of Management Education*, 3(2), 31–41.

Ramsey, C. (2005) Narrating development: Professional practice emerging within stories, *Action Research*, 3(3), 279–295.

Reason, P. (ed.) (1994) *Participation in human inquiry* (London, Sage).

Reason, P. (1999) Integrating action and reflection through co-operative inquiry, *Management Learning*, 30(2), 207–226.

Reason, P. (2006) Choice and quality in action research practice, *Journal of Management Inquiry*, 15(2), 187–203.

Reason, P. & Bradbury, H. (2001) *Handbook of action research* (London, Sage).

Reason, P. & Torbert, W. (2001) The action turn: Toward a transformational social science, *Concepts and Transformations*, 6(1), 1–37.

Revans, R. (1980) *Action learning: New techniques for management* (London, Blond & Biggs).

Schatzki, T. (2001) Introduction: Practice theory, in: T. Schatzki, K. Knorr Cetina & E. von Savigny (eds.) *The practice turn in contemporary theory* (London, Routledge), 1–14.

Schatzki, T., Knorr Cetina, K. & Savigny, E. von (eds.) (2001) *The practice turn in contemporary theory* (London, Routledge).

Shotter, J. (1993) *Conversational realities* (London, Sage).

Shotter, J. (1996) Social construction as social poetics: Oliver Sacks and the case of Dr P, in: B. Bayer & J. Shotter (eds.) *Reconstructing the psychological subject* (London, Sage), 69–83.

Shotter, J. (2000) Wittgenstein and his philosophy of beginnings and beginnings and beginnings, *Concepts and Transformations*, 5(3), 349–362.

Vygotsky, L. (1978) *Mind in society* (Cambridge, MA, Harvard University Press).

Wittgenstein, L. (1953) *Philosophical investigations*. Trans. G. Anscombe (Oxford, Basil Blackwell/Mott).

Reading 4: Soft systems methodology and action

Checkland, P. and Scholes, J. (1990) *Soft Systems Methodology in Action*, Chichester, John Wiley and Sons, pp. 1–8.

Introduction

Consider the scope of the idea of 'managing' anything. The project manager in an engineering company responsible for developing a new product, the doctor running an ear, nose and throat clinic, the single parent with a child of school age, the secretary of a trade union branch, the leader of a guerrilla band, all these are 'managers' in the broad sense of the term. To 'manage' anything in everyday life is to try to cope with a flux of interacting events and ideas which unrolls through time. The 'manager' tries to 'improve' situations which are seen as problematical – or at least as less than perfect – and the job is never done (ask the single parent!) because as the situation evolves new aspects calling for attention emerge, and yesterday's solutions may now be seen as today's 'problems'.

Soft systems methodology (SSM) helps such managers, of all kinds and at all levels, to cope with their task. It is an organized way of tackling messy situations in the real world. It is based on systems thinking, which enables it to be highly defined and described, but is flexible in use and broad in scope. The account of it here is based on the last decade of experience, and is complementary to the earlier account of SSM which described its origins and emergence, as well as the systems thinking upon which it is based and the nature of systems thinking in general (Checkland, 1981).

… [This first chapter] starts from, but does not dwell on, the basic assumptions behind SSM which make its scope so broad, and describes without going into detail the mature view, after twenty years of research, of the shape and nature of the methodology. …

Organized Purposeful Action

One of the most obvious characteristics of human beings is their readiness to attribute meaning to what they observe and experience. Indeed, human beings are not simply ready to attribute meanings, they cannot abide meaninglessness. The very existence of the world religions, and the fact that every culture develops its own myths concerning the nature of the world and our place in it, show how important it is to *homo sapiens* to create answers to the most fundamental – ultimately unanswerable – questions. Mankind finds an absence of meaning unendurable. We are a meaning-endowing animal, on both the global long-term and the local short-term level. Members of organizations, for example, tend to see the world in a particular way, to attribute at least partially shared meanings to their world. And that is equally true of corporate members of the Warsaw Pact and individual members of the Batley Ladies Sewing Circle.

Given the creation of an interpreted, not merely an experienced world, we can form *intentions*, we can decide to do one thing rather than another, in the light of how we are interpreting our situation. This seems to be a uniquely human characteristic. The chemist investigating how hydrogen and nitrogen combine to form ammonia never finds it necessary to attribute intentions to the molecules. And if we observe the behaviour of the cuckoo, though we may say casually that 'the cuckoo has the intention of laying her eggs in the nest of another bird', this is an observer's language, not meaningful to the cuckoo. To explain what is observed, we only have to assume that the cuckoo is programmed to a certain behaviour; it has not been found necessary to attribute self-consciousness to cuckoos. But to explain human behaviour, much more erratic than that of cuckoos, we need the additional concept of the 'intentions' which the human beings can formulate, act upon, and change for themselves.

Thus, on this argument, human beings cannot help attributing meaning to their experienced world; and they can then decide to do some things and not do others. They can take *purposeful action* in response to their experience of the world. By purposeful action we mean deliberate, decided, willed action, whether by an individual or by a group.

Now it would seem a good idea if purposeful action deriving from intentions were also based on knowledge rather than consisting merely of random thrashing about – though observation suggests that there may be no shortage of that in human affairs! Where might the knowledge to guide action be found? Probably the most respected source of knowledge is scientific investigation, since it produces 'public knowledge' which can be subject to public refutation (Ziman, 1968; Popper, 1963; Checkland, 1981, Chapter 2). But while the status of scientific knowledge gained in repeatable experiments concerning natural phenomena is unimpeachable in Western culture, the status of knowledge gained in the so-called social or human sciences is much less sure. This is precisely because, as Caws (1988) neatly puts it:

> The causal determinants of the objects of the social sciences always include human intentions, while those of the natural sciences do not (p. 1).

In the social sciences repeatable experiments are difficult to achieve and virtually all knowledge gained by social science is heavily meaning-bearing.

If we cannot aspire to a natural-science-like knowledge, perhaps what we seek in human affairs might be described as 'wisdom-based knowledge'. But what one observer sees as wisdom may to another be blinkered prejudice. 'Insight-based knowledge' might be another candidate, but again we have to ask: Insight in relation to whose meaning? The most neutral expression would be 'experience-based knowledge', and this accords at least with the everyday observation that we are all the time taking purposeful action in relation to our experience of the situations we find ourselves in, and the knowledge (shared or individual) which that experience yields.

This, of course, places knowledge acquisition in a cycle, namely that shown in Figure 1.1, since the purposeful action derived from experience-based knowledge will itself result in new experience. This is a cycle whose content will continually change: each time round the cycle the world experienced is a somewhat different place, and hence the cycle embodies fundamentally the possibility of *learning*. If this happens then the purposeful action can be aimed at intended improvements, that is, in the eyes of those who take the action.

The cycle of Figure 1.1 can itself be seen as the object of concern of so-called 'management science'. This is a curious field, as is indicated by problems surrounding both of the words in its name! Management science clearly ought to be relevant to managing anything in the same broad sense in which the word is being used here; in fact, management science has devoted itself almost exclusively to the concerns of only one kind of manager: professionals conducting the affairs of private and public enterprises.

Secondly, whether or not management science is a science, or whether it could or should aspire to scientific status has been much debated in the

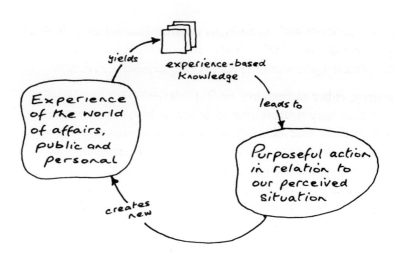

Figure 1.1 The experience-action cycle

last twenty years, as part of the wider debate about whether natural science and social science are or could be scientific in the same sense (see Checkland, 1983a, for a discussion of the management science debate in Operational Research circles, and Checkland, 1981, for discussion of the broader debate). However, these problems have not been too inhibiting to practitioners in the field. Much work has been done, and one very useful legacy from management science has been its demonstration that a particular kind of language can be very helpful in understanding and articulating the operation of the cycle of Figure 1.1. We refer to the language of systems thinking.

… In spite of the fact that there are many definitions of the word system in the literature (Jordan, 1965, p. 44–65, for example, offers fifteen) all take as given the notion of a set of elements mutually related such that the set constitutes a whole having properties as an entity. Secondly comes the crucial idea that the whole may be able to survive in a changing environment by taking control action in response to shocks from the environment. We can see at once that the cycle of Figure 1.1 can itself be viewed as 'a system', one which, if self-reflective, could learn, adapt and survive through time. So it is not surprising that systems thinking has had an important role in developing an organized approach to describing and making operational the cycle of Figure 1.1.

For that is where this argument has led us: firstly to the idea that it is probably worth trying to find ways of *formally* operating the learning cycle in which purposeful action is taken in real-world situations in order to bring about what are deemed to be improvements by those carrying out this process; and secondly to the idea that systems thinking may be helpful in this task. SSM is just such a methodology for operating the endless cycle from experience to purposeful action.

Some might deny, either in principle or from despair, that any *formal* account of the necessary process should or could be given. Surely any formal account might either be inhibiting if used prescriptively, cutting off exciting lines of thought, or inadequate if used descriptively, given the glorious richness which human beings can bring to any task? An echo of such concerns surfaced recently in a discussion in the Operational Research Society concerning the extent to which OR embodied a version of the methodology of natural science. Rivett (1989), reiterating thoughts expressed at a conference on 'Systems in OR' a few years earlier (1983), argued that formal accounts of the 'OR process' bore no relation ('complete nonsense' is Rivett's phrase) to the reality, which actually consisted of:

> A complex process which is a mixture, in practice, of fumbling, mind-changing, chaos and political intervention (p. 17).

Critics were quick to respond. Lord (1989) argued that this denied OR's 'aspiration to be a disciplined subject', that is to say, presumably, one in which critical debate can be conducted on explicit and understood premises; while Jones (1989) saw talk of the OR process as a *post hoc* effort to understand what is happening and what developments are taking place through OR work.

The authors here would argue that in SSM a process of tackling real-world problems in all their richness has been developed; that it has benefited considerably from being formally expressed, which enables lessons to be learned and also enables users to know what they are talking about; and that the particular form which SSM takes (helped here by its use of systems thinking) both enables it to be used descriptively to make sense of a complex situation, in Jones's sense, and prescriptively to control Rivett's 'chaos'. This book will seek to illustrate all these themes. Meanwhile we can define its focus using the language of the above argument: the focus is on an organized set of principles (methodology) which guide action in trying to 'manage' (in the broad sense) real-world problem situations; it is systems-thinking-based and is applicable to taking purposeful action to change real situations constructively.

The Basic Shape of SSM

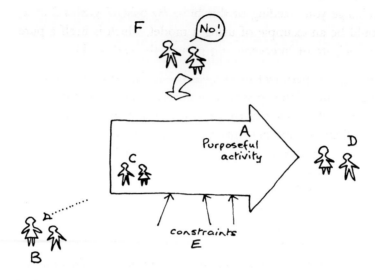

Figure 1.2 An emblematic model of purposeful activity

Let any purposeful activity be represented by an arrow (A in Figure 1.2). Such an action, being purposeful, will be an expression of the intention of some person or persons B (also Figure 1.2). Since A is a human action there will be someone (or several people) who take the action: they are C in the figure. The action will have an impact on some person or group D, and it will be taking place in an environment which may place constraints upon it. These constraints are represented by E. Finally, since human autonomy is rarely total, we can add some person or group F who could stop the action being taken. Of course in real life the same person or persons could be one or more of the elements B, C, D, F, since they are roles, not necessarily individuals or groups. Overall, Figure 1.2 is a simple emblematic model of a purposeful action; it represents one way of thinking about that concept.

Now let A be the purposeful act of you, the reader, reading this book. You are B in the figure, and could now name the other elements. For example, the nature of A could be that you are preparing for an examination in management science, or that you are satisfying a curiosity about SSM, or preparing a critique of it. Given the definitions so far you would also be element D, since reading the book will have a direct effect on you yourself. In the role F might be someone from whom you have borrowed the book, who wants it back, or you might be F yourself if the copy is your own. If someone wants the book back

within a week then that might be one of the constraints E. And so on
… It is clear that you could investigate, or prepare an account of, or
intervene to change your reading of this book by using Figure 1.2 as a
tool. This would be an example of using a model, which is itself a pure
concept, to investigate or intervene in a part of the real world.

This simple thought experiment in fact illustrates the core nature of
SSM. The basic shape of the approach is to formulate some models
which it is hoped will be relevant to the real-world situation, and use
them by setting them against perceptions of the real world in a process
of comparison. That comparison could then initiate debate leading to a
decision to take purposeful action to improve the part of real life which
is under scrutiny. In SSM the models are not quite like that in
Figure 1.2; in fact they are carefully built models of systems to carry
out purposeful activity (known as 'human activity systems') and are
somewhat more elaborate than the model used in the thought
experiment. But the principle is the same: find out about a situation in
the real world which has provoked concern; select some relevant human
activity systems; make models of them; use the models to question the
real-world situation in a comparison phase; and use the debate initiated
by the comparison to define purposeful action which would improve the
original problem situation. Taking the action would itself change the
situation, so that the whole cycle could begin again … and is in
principle never ending. (Of course your first choice of relevant system
might turn out not to be relevant. You will learn your way to true
relevance by trying out a number of models.)

The shape of SSM is thus as shown in Figure 1.3, which is a slightly
more elaborate version of Figure 1.1. Systems thinking is involved here
in two different ways, which make SSM doubly systemic. Firstly, the
process of Figure 1.3 can itself be viewed as the operation of a cyclic
learning system … ; secondly, within the process of Figure 1.3, systems
models are used to initiate and orchestrate the debate about purposeful
change. The first use of systems ideas, that the whole enquiring process
can be articulated as a system, is more fundamental than the second,
the fact that within SSM the models used to set up a comparison/
debate happen to be systems models.

… [In summary,] the argument of this introduction can be condensed
in the following way:

1   Human beings cannot help but attribute meaning to their
    perceptions of the world.

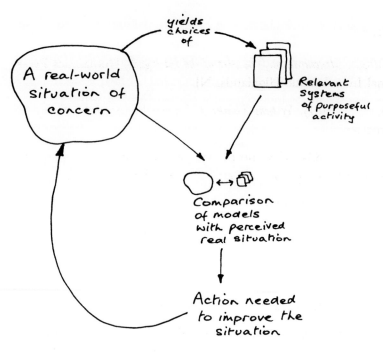

Figure 1.3 The basic shape of SSM

2 Those meanings constitute interpretations of the world which can be thought of as deriving from experience-based knowledge of the world.

3 The interpretations can inform intentions which can translate into purposeful action to improve situations perceived as lying somewhere on a scale from 'less than perfect' to 'disastrous'.

4 Purposeful action when taken changes the world as experienced (as indeed does the mental act of interpreting it) so that 1, 2, 3, above constitute a cycle.

5 The cycle can be expressed and operated by making use of systems thinking as an epistemology.

6 SSM does that in a coherent process which is itself an enquiring or learning system (and within the process uses models of purposeful activity systems).

7 SSM seeks to provide help in articulating and operating the learning cycle from meanings to intentions to purposeful action without imposing the rigidity of a technique.

References

Caws, P. (1988). *Structuralism: The Art of the Intelligible*, Humanities Press International Inc., Atlantic Highlands, NJ.

Checkland, P. B. (1981). *Systems Thinking, Systems Practice*, John Wiley & Sons, Chichester.

Checkland, P. B. (1983a). OR and the systems movement: mappings and conflicts. *Journal of the Operational Research Society*, **34**(8), 661–675.

Jones, G. (1989). Letter to *OR Newsletter*, April, 18.

Jordan, N. (1965). *Themes in Speculative Psychology*, Tavistock, London.

Kolb, D. (1984) *Experiential Learning*, Englewood Cliffs, NJ, Prentice Hall.

Lord, W. T. (1989). Letter to *OR Newsletter*, April, 18.

Popper, K. R. (1963). *Conjectures and Refutations: The Growth of Scientific Knowledge*, Routledge and Kegan Paul, London (revised edn, 1972).

Rivett, P. (1983). A world in which nothing ever happens twice. *Journal of the Operational Research Society*, **34**(8), 677–683.

Rivett, P. (1989). Letter to *OR Newsletter*, March, 17.

Ziman, J. M. (1968). *Public Knowledge: An Essay Concerning the Social Dimension of Science*, Cambridge University Press, Cambridge.

Further reading

If this introduction to reflective reading has interested you or if you would like to read more guides to reflection, I would suggest that the following books or articles might be helpful.

Melanie Jasper's book *Beginning Reflective Practice* (2003, Nelson Thornes) is excellent. Its only problem is that its intended audience is trainee nurses and so all the illustrations are to do with healthcare. However, if you can work around that then she introduces other reflective frameworks that you might find helpful. I thought that Chapters 1, 3 and 5 were particularly good.

Mike Pedlar, John Burgoyne and Tom Boydell are very well known for their work on what has been called the learning organisation. Their *Manager's Guide to Self-Development* (2001, McGraw-Hill)is a fascinating collection of exercises that you can do to help you improve your skills as a manager if that is what your work entails.

You might find it difficult to get hold of Judi Marshall's chapter from the *Handbook of Action Research*. If you do have trouble finding it, then you will be able to find a similar article in a journal held in the Open Library electronic journals collection called *Systemic Practice and Action Research*:

Marshall, J. (1999) 'Living life as inquiry', *Systemic Practice and Action Research,* vol. 12, issue 2.

Acknowledgements

Grateful acknowledgement is made to the following sources for permission to reproduce material in this book.

Text

Reading 1: Coghlan, D (2001) 'Insider action research projects: implications for practising managers', from *Management Learning*, vol. 32 issue 1. Copyright © 2001 Sage Publications Ltd. Reproduced by permission;

Reading 2: Marshall, J. (1999) 'Living life as inquiry', *Systemic Practice and Action Research*, vol. 12, no. 2, pp. 155–171. With kind permission of Springer Science and Business Media;

Reading 3: Ramsey, C. (2007) 'Ethno-experiments: creating robust inquiry and futures', *Research in Post-Compulsory Education*, 12 March 2007, pp. 377–390. Copyright © 2007 Taylor & Francis Ltd;

Reading 4: Checkland, P. and Scholes, J. (1991) 'Soft Systems Methodology and Action', *Soft Systems Methodology in Action*. Reproduced by permission of John Wiley & Sons Limited.

Illustrations

Page 15: © Reg Charity/Corbis.

Page 21: © Rainer Raffalski / Alamy.

Page 36: © www.CartoonStock.com.

Page 38: Courtesy of David Hope.

Page 71: www.CartoonStock.com.

Page 75: www.CartoonStock.com.

Page 86: www.CartoonStock.com.

Page 94: © Copyright Paperlink Limited.

Page 101: © Ken McKay/Rex Features.

Page 103: © image 100/Corbis.

Page 104: © John Birdsall.

Page 113: © Karen Parker.